Primary Sources of World Cultures™

FRANCE

A PRIMARY SOURCE CULTURAL GUIDE

Michael A. Sommers

The Rosen Publishing Group's
PowerPlus Books™
New York

Pour Annie, Tinny, Heidi, Vannie, Ronnie, Nattie, et tous, les autres

Published in 2005 by The Rosen Publishing Group, Inc.
29 East 21st Street, New York, NY 10010

Library of Congress Cataloging-in-Publication Data

Sommers, Michael A., 1966–
France: a primary source cultural guide/Michael A. Sommers.—1st ed.
  p. cm.—(Primary sources of world cultures)
Summary: An overview of the history and culture of France and its people including the geography, myths, arts, daily life, education, industry, and government, with illustrations from primary source documents. Includes bibliographical references and index.
ISBN 1-4042-2909-4 (library binding)
1. France—Juvenile literature. [1. France.] I. Title. II. Series.
DC17.S66 2005
944—dc22

                                                                      2003022270

Manufactured in the United States of America

On the cover: Children in Brittany dress up for a festival; a letter from Joan of Arc to her friend the Count of Dunois, dated March 20, 1466; a view of the Cour Napoléon (the Napoléon Court) from the Richelieu Wing at the Musée du Louvre, in Paris.

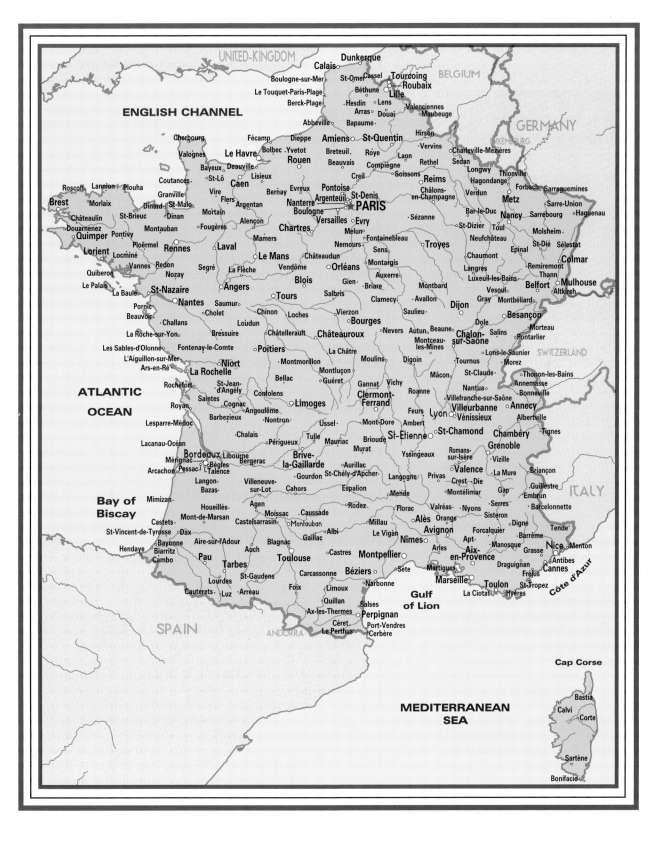

CONTENTS

INTRODUCTION

Even if you've never traveled to France, you've probably heard about it, read about it, seen photos and films of it, and perhaps even dreamed about it. Rich pastries and runny cheeses, the Eiffel Tower and the Riviera, Joan of Arc and Napoléon—the names, images, and associations are everlasting.

Ever since the Middle Ages, France has proved itself to be one of the great cradles of Western civilization. Indeed, few other nations have made such enormous contributions to world culture, literature, philosophy, art, science, music, and cuisine. The list is endless.

If it hadn't been for France and the French, who knows if today we would have such things as encyclopedias, photography, ambulances, Braille, the metric system, bicycles, batteries, hot air balloons, calculators, impressionist paintings, surrealism, haute couture, croissants, and mayonnaise. Brilliant ideas aside, France has always been one of the richest, most powerful, and most diverse nations in the world—as well as one of the leading nations of Europe.

Today, this country of more than 60 million people is a fascinating mixture of age-old traditions and cutting-edge innovations. One of the world's fastest

Paris *(left)*, population 2.2 million, is nicknamed the City of Lights. The city is divided by the Seine River into two main sections, the Left Bank and the Right Bank. At the heart of Paris is the Île de la Cité, one of two islands in the Seine. Île de la Cité is home to some of Paris's most famous historical sites such as the cathedral of Notre-Dame de Paris. Paris is the most popular tourist destination in the world. Pictured above is the front of a typical French butcher shop.

In Languedoc-Roussillon, the ruins of the walled city of Carcassone are a reminder of the rich history of France. Carcassone became a Roman town in the first century AD. However, archaeologists have found ancient artifacts that suggest the area was civilized as far back as 700 BC. The town of Carcassone, which still exists today, was founded in AD 1248. An immense amount of restoration has been done to preserve it, and it has been declared a World Heritage Site by the United Nations Educational, Scientific, and Cultural Organization (UNESCO). Visitors to Carcassone often feel as if they have walked into a medieval fairy tale.

passenger trains, the TGV, regularly hurtles past rolling hills topped with medieval stone castles. Seventeenth-century operas are performed in Paris's glittery Bastille Opera House. Made of stone and glass, it was completed in 1989. Parisians are as likely to dine on snails and raw oysters in a century-old family-run bistro as they are to stop for a quick sandwich. And while French schoolchildren learn how to construct Web sites in school, they also read the great eighteenth-century French philosophers such as Voltaire and Jean-Jacques Rousseau.

A country of immigrants, France is a nation that has always opened its arms to the world. It is also one of the most nationalistic countries on the planet. Both the French government and its citizens are fierce and proud guardians of anything viewed as typically "French"—whether it be their rich and poetic language or the crusty loaves of bread called

Bicycling is one of many favorite pastimes for French villagers as well as city dwellers. Pictured above, a woman cycles down a country lane with a baguette carefully stowed under her seat.

baguettes that are baked and sold in the traditional bakeries that can be found on nearly every street. Nowhere is this more apparent than in France's capital, Paris. One of the most beautiful cities in the world, its style, architecture, and lifestyle conjure up the very essence of what is French.

The people's strong sense of identity comes from a mixture of elements considered typically French. These include the land, people, history, literature, art, culture, food, traditions, inventions, and lifestyles of France, all of which are, at least briefly, explored in the following pages. Hopefully, by the time you reach the end of this book, you will have the curiosity and desire to further explore France on your own.

THE LAND

The Geography and Environment of France

O ne of the largest countries in Europe—in fact, the third largest in area—France is slightly bigger than the state of California. The French themselves have a nickname for their country: the hexagon. This is because it has six irregular sides: three bordered by land and three by sea.

Geography

To the northwest, the English Channel separates France from the United Kingdom, while the entire western coast is bordered by the Atlantic Ocean. To the southwest, the Pyrenees mountains create a natural frontier with Spain. South and southeast lies the Mediterranean Sea. To the east, the Alps and Jura mountains separate France from Italy and Switzerland. Meanwhile, to the northeast, France shares borders with Germany, Luxembourg, and Belgium.

Pictured at left is the popular tourist destination Chamonix, located at the foot of Mont Blanc, the tallest peak in Europe. Chamonix provides breathtaking views of the Alps. This French city hosted the first Winter Olympics in 1924. The Mont Blanc tunnel, completed in 1965, cuts through the mountain and connects Chamonix with the Italian cities of Courmayer and Val-d'Aosta. Because Mont Blanc is such a high, rocky peak, it's an attractive challenge for many mountaineers from around the globe. Pictured above is the popular and charming city of Nice, which is located on the French Riviera.

Pictured above are the rocks of Pointe du Coton at low tide. Pointe du Coton is located on the island of Belle Île en Mer, which is located just off the coast of Brittany. (Brittany is a region in western France.) Many French impressionist painters, particularly Claude Monet, have depicted Pointe du Coton in their artwork.

Mountains

In terms of geography, two-thirds of France is covered by flat plains. However, the nation is also home to two important mountain ranges: the Pyrenees and the Alps (which make France one of world's great skiing destinations). In fact, Mont Blanc, at 15,771 feet (4,807 meters), is the highest mountain in the Alps. To the east are the mountain ranges of the Ardennes, the Jura, and the Vosges. Meanwhile, the center of France is home to the Massif Central, an ancient range of volcanic mountains that covers one-sixth of the country.

Rivers

There is certainly no lack of water in France. Both flat and mountainous regions are crisscrossed by rivers. The longest of these is the Loire, which runs for 634 miles (1,020 kilometers) from the Massif Central to the Atlantic Ocean. Other major rivers include the Garonne, the Rhône, the Rhine, and the Seine, which horizontally splits the city of Paris in half.

Coastline

France also boasts 2,129 miles (3,427 km) of coastline. To the north are the icy waters of the North Sea and the English Channel. To the west are the rough seas and wild sandy dunes of the Atlantic Ocean. To the south are the bluffs and mostly pebbly beaches that are lapped by the warm turquoise waters of the Mediterranean Sea.

Regions of France

Centuries ago, when France was a monarchy ruled by kings, the country was divided up into thirty-seven provinces, some of which were tiny kingdoms controlled by local dukes and counts. The province of Burgundy, for instance—today known for its famous wines—used to be a small kingdom ruled by the Duke of Burgundy. Île-de-France, with Paris as its capital, was ruled by the Capetian kings.

Pictured above is the village of Beaujolais, nestled in an area of the same name, Pays de Beaujolais (Beaujolais country). Pays de Beaujolais is known for its wine. The region has twelve different wine districts. These districts are protected by the government because they each possess a unique set of variables (soil, surrounding plants, vines), which contribute to the production of a wine that cannot be replicated elsewhere. Most famous is Beaujolais Nouveau (new Beaujolais), which is drunk very soon after the grapes are harvested and for a short time only.

Over time, many of these provinces developed their own traditions, architecture, style of dress, and music. Some, such as Brittany, Normandy, and Corsica, even had their own languages. In fact, it took more than a thousand years and the determination of French kings and then presidents to unify all these regions into the single nation of France that exists today.

After the French Revolution, these provinces were replaced by departments in order to make it easier to govern the country. In 1790, there were eighty-three departments. Today, there are ninety-six. There are also four overseas departments (*département d'outre-mer*; DOMs): the two Caribbean islands of Guadeloupe and Martinique, the South American territory of French Guiana, and the island of La Réunion, located in the Indian Ocean, off the southeast coast of Africa. Although far away from continental (i.e., European) France, these four territories are governed in the exact same way as the rest of France. Their residents are French citizens with the same rights and privileges as French living in Paris or Marseilles.

France also possesses overseas territories (*territoires d'outre-mer*; TOMs). These include the islands of French Polynesia, New Caledonia, Wallis, and Futuna—all located in the South Pacific—and the French Southern and Antarctic Territories. Two other island territories, Mayotte (in the Indian Ocean) and the islands of Saint Pierre and Miquelon (off the coast of Newfoundland), have special status.

In 1955, France was divided into twenty-two geographic regions. Many of these regions' borders were based on those of the traditional provinces. Today, when people talk about visiting or traveling throughout France, they refer to these regions—for example, Alsace-Lorraine, Aquitaine, Burgundy, or Languedoc-Roussillon.

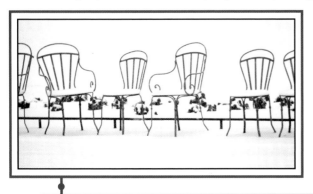

Climate

Overall, France has a fairly mild climate with four distinct seasons. The biggest differences in weather occur between the north and the south. In northern France, the only regions where the winters get quite cold are in the northeast

Shown above is a snowy winter scene in the famous Luxembourg Gardens in Paris. Though winters in the country's capital are damp, snow is not a frequent sight. The Luxembourg Gardens, which were built in 1610, are a favorite place for Parisians to relax and read when the weather is nice. Pictured at right is a historic map of France divided into fifty-eight provinces. The map was created by French cartographer Louis-Charles in 1765. It is now housed in the Bibliothéque Nationale in Paris.

Pink flamingoes are a common sight in the wildlife reserve of La Camargue, located south of Arles. Because Camargue is situated between two arms of the Rhône delta, it provides a diverse environment for many types of plant and animal life.

and in the mountains. In the northwest, the nearness of the Atlantic Ocean creates high humidity, strong westerly winds, and lots of rain. However, the temperature rarely goes below freezing. Meanwhile, throughout the north, summers can become hot, particularly in July and August.

The south boasts a much more Mediterranean climate, meaning that it receives a lot more sun. Most of the rain that does fall is limited to sudden spring and autumn downpours. The one unpleasant aspect of this climate is a wind called the mistral. The mistral is a very fierce cold and dry wind that blows through the Rhône Valley, particularly in the spring. At times it is so strong and shrill (it often howls and shrieks) that people blame it for making them feel upset or irritated.

Environment and Wildlife

France's great geographic and climactic variety is responsible for a rich array of plant and animal life. Farmland and forests currently cover 82 percent of the total area of France. And more than one-fifth of France is still covered with forest—mostly oak, beech, and pine trees. In fact, after

The chamois, a hollow-horned mountain goat, lives in the Alps and the Pyrenees mountains. The chamois' rubber-like hooves and ability to make steep jumps allow the animal to live in mountainous environments. As well, the chamois grows a thick coat that helps it retain warmth during cold winter months at high altitudes.

A European beaver, known in France as *castor d'Europe*, gathers food for its young. Beavers were once common in Europe. However, due to the demand for beaver pelts, they were nearly driven to extinction by the mid-nineteenth century. In recent years, the European beaver has begun to reappear, particularly around the Rhine River.

Sweden and Finland, France has more forest than any other country in western Europe.

For a European country, France has a surprising variety of trees—136 different kinds, to be precise. Sadly, in late 1999, fierce storms uprooted more than 60 million of them. Although the storm was a great natural catastrophe, a vast replanting program is underway. The forests, along with wetlands such as bogs and marshes, are home to a small but diverse array of wildlife ranging from chamois and *bouquetins* (two types of wild mountain goats) to beavers and storks. Other native creatures include brown bears, wolves, otters, and Corsican deer. Unfortunately, the spread of farming, the growth of cities, wildfires, and increased pollution have brought these rare mammals close to extinction.

In order to preserve France's natural heritage, the government has established 7 national parks, 137 nature reserves, 463 designated areas for protected animal species, and 389 protected coastal areas. France also has 32 regional nature parks covering more than 7 percent of the country.

Early on December 26, 1999, what became known as *la grande tempête* (the big storm) hit Paris, with winds reaching 118 miles per hour (190 km/h). As a result, many trees fell, windows broke, and the Seine overflowed.

DÉCLARATION DES DROITS DE L'HOMME ET DU CITOYEN,

Décretés par l'Assemblée Nationale dans les séances des 20, 21, 23, 24 et 26 août 1789, acceptés par le Roi.

PRÉAMBULE

LES représentans du peuple François, constitués en assemblée nationale, considérant que l'ignorance, l'oubli ou le mépris des droits de l'homme sont les seules causes des malheurs publics et de la corruption des gouvernemens ont résolu d'exposer dans une déclaration solemnelle, les droits naturels, inaliénables et sacrés de l'homme, afin que cette déclaration, constamment présente à tous les membres du corps social, leur rappelle sans cesse leurs droits et leurs devoirs, afin que les actes du pouvoir législatif et ceux du pouvoir exécutif, pouvant être à chaque instant comparés avec le but de toute institution politique, en soient plus respectés; afin que les reclamations des citoyens, fondées désormais sur des principes simples et incontestables, tournent toujours au maintien de la constitution et du bonheur de tous.

EN conséquence, l'assemblée nationale reconnoit et déclare, en présence et sous les auspices de l'Etre suprême les droits suivans de l'homme et du citoyen.

ARTICLE PREMIER.

LES hommes naissent et demeurent libres et égaux en droits, les distinctions sociales ne peuvent être fondées que sur l'utilité commune.

II.

LE but de toute association politique est la conservation des droits naturels et inprescriptibles de l'homme; ces droits sont la liberté, la propriété, la sureté, et la résistance à l'oppression.

III.

LE principe de toute souveraineté réside essentiellement dans la nation, nul corps, nul individu ne peut exercer d'autorité qui n'en émane expressément.

IV.

LA liberté consiste à pouvoir faire tout ce qui ne nuit pas à autrui Ainsi, l'exercice des droits naturels de chaque homme, n'a de bornes que celles qui assurent aux autres membres de la société la jouissance de ces mêmes droits; ces bornes ne peuvent être déterminées que par la loi.

V.

LA loi n'a le droit de défendre que les actions nuisibles à la société, Tout ce qui n'est pas défendu par la loi ne peut être empêché, et nul ne peut être contraint à faire ce qu'elle n'ordonne pas.

VI.

LA loi est l'expression de la volonté générale; tous les citoyens ont droit de concourir personnellement, ou par leurs représentans, à sa formation; elle doit être la même pour tous, soit qu'elle protege, soit qu'elle punisse. Tous les citoyens étant égaux à ses yeux, sont également admissibles à toutes dignités, places et emplois publics, selon leur capacité, et sans autres distinction que celles de leurs vertus et de leurs talens.

VII.

NUL homme ne peut être accusé, arrêté, ni détenu que dans les cas déterminés par la loi, et selon les formes qu'elle a prescrites, ceux qui sollicitent, expédient, exécutent ou font exécuter des ordres arbitraires, doivent être punis; mais tout citoyen appelé ou saisi en vertu de la loi, doit obéir à l'instant, il se rend coupable par la résistance.

VIII.

LA loi ne doit établir que des peines scrictement et évidemment nécessaire, et nul ne peut être puni qu'en vertu d'une loi établie, et promulguée antérieurement au délit, et légalement appliquée.

IX.

TOUT homme étant présumé innocent jusqu'à ce qu'il ait été déclaré coupable, s'il est jugé indispensable de l'arrêter, toute rigueur qui ne serait pas nécessaire pour s'assurer de sa personne doit être sévèrement réprimée par la loi.

X.

NUL ne doit être inquieté pour ses opinions, mêmes religieuses, pourvu que leur manifestation ne trouble pas l'ordre public établi par la loi.

XI.

LA libre communication des pensées et des opinions est un des droits les plus precieux de l'homme; tout citoyen peut donc parler écrire, imprimer librement; sauf à répondre de l'abus de cette liberté dans les cas déterminés par la loi.

XII.

LA garantie des droits de l'homme et du citoyen nécessite une force publique; cette force est donc instituée pour l'avantage de tous, et non pour l'utilité particuliere de ceux à qui elle est confiée.

XIII.

POUR l'entretien de la force publique, et pour les dépenses d'administration, une contribution commune est indispensable; elle doit être également répartie entre les citoyens en raison de leurs facultées.

XIV.

LES citoyens ont le droit de constater par eux même ou par leurs représentans, la nécessité de la contribution publique, de la consentir librement, d'en suivre l'emploi, et d'en déterminer la quotité, l'assiette, le recouvrement et la durée.

XV.

LA société a le droit de demander compte à tout agent public de son administration.

XVI.

TOUTE société, dans laquelle la garantie des droits n'est pas assurée, ni la séparation des pouvoirs déterminée, n'a point de constitution.

XVII.

LES propriétés étant un droit inviolable et sacré, nul ne peut en être privé, si ce n'est lorsque la nécessité publique, légalement constatée, l'exige évidemment, et sous la condition d'une juste et préalable indemnité.

AUX REPRESENTANS DU PEUPLE FRANCOIS

THE PEOPLE

2

The Ancient Gauls and the Modern French

The earliest traces of humans to be found on the territory that became known as France date back to 90,000 BC. However, the first records of a human civilization date back to around 25,000 BC, when a Stone Age people known as Cro-Magnons developed a sophisticated culture in this area.

Early Civilizations

The cave-dwelling Cro-Magnons lived in the hills of southwest France. They left beautiful paintings on the walls of the region's caverns, which can still be seen today. The most famous of these is the Lascaux cave located in the Dordogne region.

As centuries passed, groups of farmers and herders spread throughout the country. Between 2000 and 1500 BC, the first Celts came from central Europe to northwest France. The Celts were known as Gauls. Their territory (what are now France and Belgium) was also called Gaul by the Romans, who, in 58 BC, decided to conquer the country and add it to the Roman Empire.

UNITE·INDIVISIBILITE
DE LA RÉPUBLIQUE
LIBERTE · EGALITE
FRATERNITE OU LA MORT

At left is a painting of the Declaration of the Rights of Man and of the Citizen. The rights were written on August 26, 1789, as a response to the French Revolution. Very similar to the American Bill of Rights, this French document outlines basic freedoms, such as the right to vote. Above is a poster from 1792, which states the motto for the new French Republic, "Liberty, Equality and Brotherhood or Death." Many similar posters were displayed in France after the revolution to remind the public of their new government's values.

The Gauls and Romans

Although the Romans believed they were primitive wild men, the scraggly haired Gauls were far from uncivilized. The Gauls invented soap and wooden barrels. They made ornate jewelry out of gold and traveled in carts with metal wheels. However, after years of conflict, the Gauls' chief, Vercingetorix, was defeated by Julius Caesar in 52 BC.

Gaul became a province of Rome, and the Gauls became Roman citizens. Over the next few centuries, the Gauls farmed and traded the many objects they made. They were exposed to Roman culture, learned to speak Latin, and converted to Christianity. They traveled on Roman-built roads (some of which still exist) and worked and lived in Roman-built cities such as Lutetia (Paris) and Lugdunum (Lyon). In many ancient French cities such as Arles, Marseilles, and even Paris, the ruins of Roman buildings and monuments are still standing.

The Franks

The Roman Empire began its decline in the third century. In the fifth century, Germanic groups from the east began to invade Gaul. The most powerful of these invaders were the Franks, from which the name "France" originated. The king of the Franks, Clovis, was crowned as the first king of France in 485. He became the first king of the Merovingian dynasty. This was France's first royal family in which power was passed from father to son. Clovis converted to Christianity and succeeded in unifying most of Gaul. In 507, he made the tiny trading town of Paris into the capital of France.

Over time, the Merovingian dynasty became weak. In 732, the king's chancellor, Charles Martel, was responsible for turning back Arabic Muslims who had invaded France from Spain. In 754, Martel's son, Pépin, had himself crowned king by the pope. This was the beginning of the Carolingian dynasty and of the idea of

Pictured at left are prehistoric menhirs left behind by the ancient Celts who once inhabited Brittany. The menhirs, which are numerous (more than 3,000), are located in Carnac, a coastal town in Brittany. The purpose of the Carnac stones remains unknown. However, some historians think that the monuments were prehistoric calendars used by the druids. Above is an anonymous medieval painting from the fourteenth century depicting the baptism of Clovis I, the first king of France. He converted to Christianity.

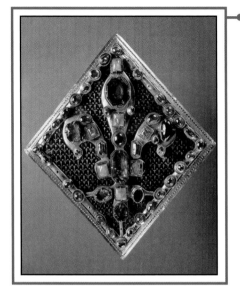

The fleur-de-lys (lily)—a symbol of France and French royalty—was a typical design in royal jewelry, particularly during the Middle Ages. This gold and jewelled brooch supposedly belonged to Louis IX. He ruled from 1226 to 1270.

divine monarchy—in which the king was seen as a direct link to God.

Pépin's son, Charlemagne, expanded his control over all of Gaul and, soon after, much of Europe. In 800, he was crowned emperor of the Holy Roman Empire, an area that included present-day France, Germany, and Italy. However, when Charlemagne died, the Holy Roman Empire and France split into tiny kingdoms ruled by local counts and dukes. By the time the last Carolingian king died in 987, the French monarchy (based in Paris) was very weak.

The Capetians

In 987, many local French lords elected Hugh Capet to be their king. This was the beginning of the Capetian dynasty, which ruled France until the 1300s. Under the Capetians, France became the greatest power in Europe, and Paris became an influential capital. All of the important decisions concerning the French kingdom were made in Paris.

This painting shows French knights leaving a castle for a tournament. The painting was done during the latter half of the fifteenth century. The work is believed to be inspired by the tales of Froissart, a French historian who chronicled the Hundred Years' War.

A late fifteenth-century German tapestry celebrates Joan of Arc's arrival at the Château de Chinon in 1428. At Chinon, Joan was asked to find King Charles, who was disguised as a member of his royal court. He thought that if she could identify him, she must truly be on a mission from God.

Throughout the Middle Ages, however, France had one great problem: England. The conflicts over territory between the two kingdoms led to the Hundred Years' War (1337–1453), in which both countries fought for control of France. It was thanks to the courage of a farm girl named Joan of Arc (Jeanne d' Arc) that French soldiers succeeded in expelling English invaders from France. In 1429, seventeen-year-old Joan helped drive the English from the captured town of Orleans. She claimed she was guided by the voices of saints, but her enemies thought she was a witch. Eventually, she was betrayed and handed over to the English, who burned her at the stake.

A letter dated March 20, 1431, from Joan of Arc to her friend the Count of Dunois. During Dunois's battles against the English, Joan advised him about the attacks he planned in Normandy. Because many believed that Joan was inspired by God, her battle plans were rarely questioned.

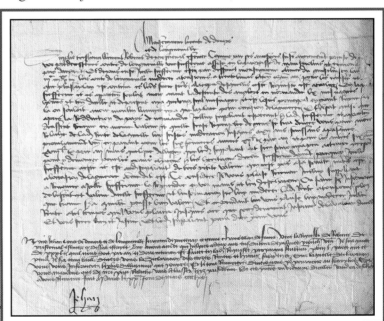

King François I was responsible for importing and commissioning work from several important Italian Renaissance painters and artists such as Titian, Michelangelo, Raphael, and Leonardo da Vinci. However, this portrait of François I was completed in 1530 by the French-Flemish painter Jean Clouet, whose work was also inspired by the Italian Renaissance.

The Renaissance

With England no longer a threat, France prospered during the early 1500s. King François I was a great art lover. He hired various great Italian Renaissance artists to come to France. Many of the artists built splendid palaces, or châteaux, particularly in the Loire Valley region, where the king himself lived.

In the mid-1500s, conflicts occurred between the growing number of Huguenots (French Protestants) and Catholics. This led to the Wars of Religion, a series of bloody battles fought among members of both religions. The violence continued until 1589, when Henri of Navarre was crowned Henri IV, king of France. Henri IV ended the Wars of Religion and stabilized the country when he signed the Edict of Nantes in 1598. This edict was a written command that guaranteed religious freedom to all French citizens.

The Seventeenth Century—Absolute Monarchy

In the seventeenth century, France became increasingly wealthy and influential while the French kings became all-powerful. Known as absolute monarchs, the kings ruled as if they were gods. Between 1610 and 1643, Louis XIII and his minister, Cardinal Richelieu, increased the power of the French court while reducing the authority of the local lords who ruled over small regions. Important colonies in Africa, North America, and the West Indies supplied France with valuable items, ranging from furs and sugar to gemstones and precious woods. These new resources poured into the country, making France a rich nation.

At right is a full-length portrait of Louis XIV that was completed in 1701 by French painter Hyacinthe Rigaud. During the reign of Louis XIV, Rigaud was the most important portraitist working in France. His work was admired for its portrayal of the luxury that marked the era.

The Palace of Versailles was completed in 1688 by architect Louis Le Vau. The fabulous gardens were designed by André Le Notré. Louis XIV entertained much of France's nobility here. Versailles was a costly palace to maintain. Historians think that approximately 25 percent of France's budget went to finance the gigantic château. Pictured here is the famous Hall of Mirrors. This is the largest room in the palace. It is lined with seventeen mirrors on one side and seventeen windows on the other.

Louis XIII was followed by Louis XIV, who was king from 1643 to 1715. His influence was so great that he was known as the Sun King. Like Louis XIII, Louis XIV had two ministers who helped him govern: Cardinal Mazarin and, later, Cardinal Colbert. During his reign, Louis XIV built a splendid court outside Paris, in the town of Versailles. With its extravagant decor, endless banquets, and dozens of brilliant court writers, musicians, and artists, Versailles became famous throughout Europe. At the same time, the Sun King became the most glamorous and powerful leader the continent had ever known.

Louis XIV also loved military glory. During his reign, he went to war against most of Europe. His dreams were so grand, however, that before long he had overextended himself. France began to lose battles. In fact, by the end of his reign, the nation was on the verge on bankruptcy due to so many costly wars.

This colored lithograph depicts a battle scene during the storming of the Bastille on July 14, 1789. The image was published in 1889 to mark the 100th anniversary of one of the most important events in French history.

Revolution

The successors of the Sun King, Louis XV and Louis XVI, had to struggle with the growing resentment of their citizens, who demanded more rights.

As a result of war, France lost important colonies in North America and India to England. Financial problems led the court to increase taxes. This unfair measure only deepened people's anger against the monarchy.

The resentment grew, and on July 14, 1789, hundreds of armed Parisians invaded the Bastille, a prison that was a symbol of the French kings' unjust rule. This event marked the beginning of the French Revolution. Throughout the countryside, peasants attacked aristocratic lords' châteaux.

A calendar marking the second year of the French Republic reads "Unity, Indivisibility of the Republic, Liberty, Equality, Brotherhood or Death." This calendar was used for thirteen years until it was abolished by Napoléon in 1804 because it excluded the Catholic Sabbath.

DÉCRET

DE L'ASSEMBLÉE NATIONALE.

Du trois Septembre 1791.

La Constitution française.

Déclaration des droits de l'homme et du Citoyen.

Les Représentans du Peuple Français, constitués en Assemblée Nationale, considérant que l'ignorance, l'oubli ou le mépris des droits de l'homme sont les seules causes des malheurs publics et de la Corruption des Gouvernemens, ont résolu d'exposer, dans une Déclaration solennelle, les droits naturels, inaliénables et sacrés de l'homme, afin que cette déclaration, constamment présente à tous les Membres du Corps social, leur rappelle sans cesse leurs droits et leurs devoirs ; afin que les actes du pouvoir Législatif et ceux du pouvoir

In August, the Declaration of the Rights of Man and of the Citizen was written and adopted. The document included the famous French concepts of *Liberté, Egalité, et Fraternité* (Liberty, Equality, and Brotherhood), which all French citizens treasure to this day. Both the revolution and the declaration served as inspirations to many other countries and their politicians—for example, to Thomas Jefferson, when he wrote the United States' Declaration of Independence.

In 1792, Louis XVI and his extravagant wife, Marie Antoinette, were thrown into jail. For a while, France was controlled by a mild group of revolutionaries known as the Girondists. However, there was fighting between the Girondists and the more radical revolutionaries, the Jacobins. Eventually, the Jacobins seized control of France. They declared the First Republic—the first of France's five democratic governments, each with its own constitution. Led by three radicals, Robespierre, Danton, and Marat, the chaotic Reign of Terror began and was characterized by mass executions, bloody street battles, and much fear.

In 1793, Louis XVI and Marie Antoinette were executed by guillotine, as were many others at Place de la Révolution (today, Place de la Concorde) in the center of Paris. Murders and executions continued to claim many lives, including those of many Jacobin leaders. Finally, in 1794, even Robespierre himself was guillotined for his bloody practices.

After King Louis XVI attempted to escape to Germany, he was captured by a group of revolutionaries and returned to France. Pictured at left is the Constitution of 1791, which declared the separation of church and state. Louis XVI was forced by the French people to sign this constitution. His signature appears in the left-hand margin of the document. He served as a constitutional monarch for only a year until he and his wife, Marie Antoinette, were arrested and beheaded on January 21, 1793. Above is a 1793 print depicting the beheading of Marie Antoinette. Marie Antoinette's strong political influence over her husband is said to have been a major reason why the once popular Louis XVI fell out of favor with the French.

At left is one of Jacques-Louis David's greatest paintings, *Napoléon Crossing Mount Saint Bernard* (1810), which shows a battle-ready Napoléon atop his horse. Below is Napoléon and Josephine's marriage certificate, dated April 2, 1810. It is signed by members of the imperial family. Napoléon and Josephine are one of history's most famous couples.

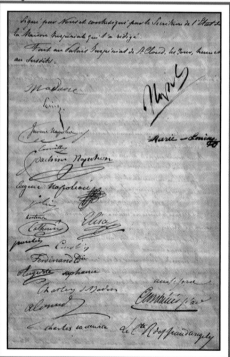

Napoléon Bonaparte

The Reign of Terror came to an end in 1799 when a brilliant young general named Napoléon Bonaparte arrived in Paris determined to restore order. A great politician and popular leader, he quickly rose to power. In 1804, he crowned himself Emperor Napoléon I.

Napoléon set up a strong central government and a strict new code of law. He created the Bank of France and the entire French administrative system. Eager for military glory, he waged wars and, for a while, succeeded in conquering most of Europe. However, two major defeats led to the end of his empire and his downfall. In 1812, Napoléon's troops were defeated in Russia, and in 1815, he surrendered to the English during the Battle of Waterloo. Afterward, he was exiled from France and spent the rest of his days on the tiny Atlantic island of St. Helena.

The Nineteenth Century

Napoléon was replaced by the heir to the French royal family, Louis XVIII. Louis XVIII created a moderate constitutional monarchy but was overthrown by Charles X, who installed a more absolute style of monarchy.

Not surprisingly, this return to a pre-revolutionary form of monarchy didn't please the French citizens. The Revolution of 1830 forced Charles X to step down as king. He was replaced in 1831 by Louis Philippe (Duke of Orleans). Elected to power by the French people themselves, he became known as the Citizen King. During his reign, the North African territory of Algeria became a French colony. However, in the 1840s, economic crises and the government's refusal to give the vote to the middle class led to the Revolution of 1848.

The result of this revolution was the creation of what was called the Second Republic. Shortly after, Napoléon's nephew, Louis Napoléon Bonaparte, was voted into power as France's first president. In 1852, he was crowned Emperor Napoléon III. Napoléon III did much to modernize France. He hired Baron Haussmann to redesign Paris into a modern city of grand avenues. He spurred on France's industrial revolution. He also supported social reforms such as laws that gave all male citizens the right to vote and all workers the right to strike.

However, trouble occurred when Napoléon III led France into the Franco-Prussian War of 1870 against Germany. When France lost the war to Germany, along with the provinces of Alsace and a part of Lorraine, Napoléon III was sent into exile. Never again would France have a king. The year 1870 marked the beginning of the Third Republic and a series of governments led by democratically elected presidents.

World War I and the Popular Front

In 1914, World War I broke out in Europe. Shortly after, Germany invaded France. Many battles took place in

The Eiffel Tower, named after its architect, Gustave Eiffel, was commissioned by the French government as an entranceway to the Paris Exposition of 1889. In 2002, the Eiffel Tower received its 200 millionth visitor. This photograph of the landmark tower was taken in July 1888 after the completion of the tower's second level.

trenches on French soil. By the time the war ended in 1918, it had devastated the country. More than 25 percent of the 8 million French soldiers who fought in the war were killed or injured. Many factories and farms were destroyed.

The Depression of the 1930s hit France hard. Unemployed and struggling workers demanded more rights from the government. Two political parties from the Left—the Socialists and the Communists—joined forces to form the Front Populaire (Popular Front). In l936, its leader, Léon Blum, became president. His government gave more rights to workers, including increased wages, a forty-hour workweek, and paid vacations.

World War II

In 1939, World War II broke out, and the following year, Adolf Hitler's German forces invaded France. The German

Shortly after the Nazis took control of France, Hitler visited Paris. When news of his arrival reached Paris, workers at the Eiffel Tower dismantled the elevators so the Nazi dictator would have to climb the steps to the top. Hitler ended up not climbing the tower. In this photograph, Hitler *(second from right)* and his company walk in front of the famous tower on July 15, 1940.

Soon after de Gaulle's famous radio broadcast, "The Appeal of June 18, 1940," he was sentenced to four years in prison. The *Paris-Soir* newspaper dated August 4, 1940, is headlined "General Charles de Gaulle condemned to death by a new military tribunal." De Gaulle hid in London. There, he led the Resistance movement of the French people against the Nazi occupation.

Nazis occupied Paris and northern and western France. A French military officer, Marshall Pétain, formed the pro-Nazi government that controlled southern France. Many French, including a large group of Communists, joined the Resistance movement that opposed the Germans and sought to free France.

General Charles de Gaulle led the Resistance movement from London. Representing the free French government, he joined forces with English prime minister Winston Churchill and U.S. president Franklin Delano Roosevelt to defeat the Nazis. In 1944, de Gaulle's French troops accompanied British and American forces in the D-day military operation that led to the liberation of France from the Germans.

France emerged from the war bankrupt and devastated by heavy bombing. A new constitution was written, and the Fourth Republic was declared. Women were given the right to vote, and the beginning of France's generous welfare program was put into place. Despite its war wounds, France prospered in the 1950s as a result of mass industrialization. It went from being a largely agricultural nation to a modern, industrial one.

In a photograph dated May 13, 1959, Muslim women in Algeria express support for France by carrying banners with pictures of Charles de Gaulle. Until the end of the Algerian war in 1962, Algerians were divided in their attitudes toward France. Since gaining its independence in 1962, Algeria has been troubled by civil war.

Colonial Wars and Social Change

In 1958, France entered the Fifth Republic. General Charles de Gaulle was elected prime minister and, later, president. Although he tried to maintain France's traditional image of grandeur and glory, social problems in the 1960s made it difficult for him to govern.

During the late 1950s and early 1960s, France had to deal with its colonies in Asia and Africa that were seeking independence. The French fought wars in Vietnam and in Algeria, where locals rebelled against French forces and colonists who opposed their desire for independence. During these wars, many colonists of French origin sought refuge in France. These immigrants—particularly those from Algeria and other

French students, protesting the old-fashioned systems of education and government in France, rally in the streets and use overturned cars as barricades against the police. Conflicts between police and students were common during the late 1960s in France. This photograph was taken in Paris on May 11, 1968.

African (particularly Muslim) countries—were sometimes victims of racist attitudes.

Immigrants and workers, women, and students became increasingly dissatisfied with de Gaulle's conservative government. In 1968, students took to the streets of Paris in violent protests against an out-of-date education system. Workers, women, and many other professionals joined in nationwide protests and strikes. Their actions shut down the country but signaled the beginning of a change in values and institutions ranging from schools to government agencies. The following year, de Gaulle resigned.

Contemporary France

In the 1970s, France became more liberal and modernized. This change of attitude resulted in the Socialist Party's return to power for the first time since Léon Blum. In 1981, President François Mitterrand headed a government that promised to tax the

A photograph taken in May 1968 shows a mob of angry students shouting at French policemen during a riot in Paris. Ultimately, 10 million workers and students went on strike.

French protesters gather together in an anti–Le Pen demonstration on May 1, 2002. Jean-Marie Le Pen is the president of the National Front political party, which he founded in 1972. Le Pen has been a candidate for the French presidency many times. He continues to be a highly controversial political figure.

rich, create more welfare for the poor, give more power to local governments, and give more rights, including French citizenship, to immigrants.

Meanwhile, a big drop in the French birth rate and an increase in Arab and African immigrants from former French colonies led some French people to worry that the country was being overrun by foreigners. Racist attitudes were stirred up by the Far Right National Front (NF) Party, whose leader, Jean-Marie Le Pen, gained popularity by taking a strong anti-immigrant position.

Mitterrand also supported a joined union of European nations that would be bound together politically and economically. In 1992, French citizens voted whether they wanted to join the European Union (EU) of fifteen other nations. (The EU is discussed in more detail at the end of chapter 11.) In a vote that split the country in half, 49 percent of the population voted "no," while 51 percent voted "yes."

In the 1990s, the government was spending great amounts of money on public projects. Meanwhile, unemployment rose, poverty and crime increased, and

Current French president Jacques Chirac poses for a picture in April 2002. Before becoming the president in 1995, Chirac was the mayor of Paris from 1977 until 1995. He also served as a French prime minister twice; once from 1974 to 1976 and again from 1986 to 1988.

homeless people were living in city streets. These major economic problems resulted in the Socialists losing power in 1995.

The new president was Jacques Chirac, the former mayor of Paris and a founder of the right-wing Rally for the Republic party (Rassemblement Pour La République; RPR). Shortly after Chirac's election, bombings by Islamist terrorists in Paris and Lyon increased racial conflicts. New laws were passed that made it more difficult for foreigners to enter the country and become French citizens. Meanwhile, other new laws were created that made it easier for immigrants—both legal and illegal—to be deported from France.

In 2002, the French franc, France's national currency, was removed from circulation. Along with eleven other EU nations, France had a new currency: the Euro. Today, the French borders are open to citizens of other EU nations. While fiercely proud of its past and its many regional traditions, France increasingly embraces the different peoples and cultures that are slowly changing its population.

...OV..............DIVVS AVG................................ET PATRVV STI
CAESAR OMNIVM FLOREM VBIQVE COLONIARVM AC MVNICIPIORVM BO
NORVM SCILICET VIRORVM ET LOCVPLETIVM IN HAC CVRIA ESSE VOLVIT
QVID ERGO NON ITALICVS SENATOR PROVINCIALI POTIOR EST · IAM
VOBIS CVM HANC PARTEM CENSVRAE MEAE ADPROBARE COEPERO QVID
DE EA RE SENTIAM REBVS OSTENDAM · SED NE PROVINCIALES QVIDEM
SI MODO ORNARE CVRIAM POTERINT REICIENDOS PVTO
ORNATISSIMA ECCE COLONIA VALENTISSIMAQVE VIENNENSIVM QVAM
LONGO IAM TEMPORE SENATORES HVIC CVRIAE CONFERT EX QVA COLO
NIA INTER PAVCOS EQVESTRIS ORDINIS ORNAMENTVM L VESTINVM FA
MILIARISSIME DILIGO ET HODIEQVE IN REBVS MEIS DETINEO CVIVS LIBE
RI FRVANTVR QVAESO PRIMO SACERDOTIORVM GRADV POSTMODO CVM
ANNIS PROMOTVRI DIGNITATIS SVAE INCREMENTA VT DIRVM NOMEN LA
TRONIS TACEAM ET ODI ILLVD PALAESTRICVM PRODIGIVM QVOD ANTE IN DO
MVM CONSVLATVM INTVLIT QVAM COLONIA SVA SOLIDVM CIVITATIS ROMA
NAE BENIFICIVM CONSECVTA EST · IDEM DE FRATRE EIVS POSSVM DICERE
MISERABILI QVIDEM INDIGNISSIMOQVE HOC CASV VT VOBIS VTILIS
SENATOR ESSE NON POSSIT
TEMPVS EST IAM TI CAESAR GERMANICE DETEGERE TE PATRIBVS CONSCRIPTIS
QVO TENDAT ORATIO TVA IAM ENIM AD EXTREMOS FINES GALLIAE NAR
BONENSIS VENISTI
TOT ECCE INSIGNES IVVENES QVOT INTVEOR NON MAGIS SVNT PAENITENDI
SENATORES QVAM PAENITET PERSICVM NOBILISSIMVM VIRVM AMI
CVM MEVM INTER IMAGINES MAIORVM SVORVM ALLOBROGICI NO
MEN LEGERE QVOD SI HAEC ITA ESSE CONSENTITIS QVID VLTRA DESIDERA
TIS QVAM VT VOBIS DIGITO DEMONSTREM SOLVM IPSVM VLTRA FINES
PROVINCIAE NARBONENSIS IAM VOBIS SENATORES MITTERE QVANDO
EX LVGVDVNO HABERE NOS NOSTRI ORDINIS VIROS NON PAENITET
TIMIDE QVIDEM P C EGRESSVS ADSVETOS FAMILIARESQVE VOBIS PRO
VINCIARVM TERMINOS SVM · SED DESTRICTE IAM COMATAE GALLIAE
CAVSA AGENDA EST · IN QVA SI QVIS HOC INTVETVR QVOD BELLO PER DE
CEM ANNOS EXERCVERVNT DIVOM IVLIVM IDEM OPPONAT CENTVM
ANNORVM IMMOBILEM FIDEM OBSEQVIVMQVE MVLTIS TREPIDIS RE
BVS NOSTRIS PLVS QVAM EXPERTVM ILLI PATRI MEO DRVSO GERMANIAM
SVBIGENTI TVTAM QVIETE SVA SECVRAMQVE A TERGO PACEM PRAES
TITERVNT ET QVIDEM CVM AD CENSVS NOVO TVM OPERE ET IN ADSVE
TO GALLIS AD BELLVM AVOCATVS ESSET QVOD OPVS QVAM AR
DVVM SIT NOBIS NVNC CVM MAXIME QVAMVIS NIHIL VLTRA QVAM
VT PVBLICE NOTAE SINT FACVLTATES NOSTRAE EXQVIRATVR · NIMIS
MAGNO EXPERIMENTO COGNOSCIMVS

THE LANGUAGES OF FRANCE

3

From Celtic, Latin, and Romance to Modern French

I n the period in which France was known as Gaul, Celtic was the language that was spoken the most. However, with the Roman invasion of Gaul, Latin—the language of the Roman Empire—spread throughout Gaul. Latin is the base of many Romance languages, including Italian, Spanish, Portuguese, and French. In Gaul, Latin became the main spoken language until the fifth century.

Origins of the French Language

By AD 500, the Roman Empire had fallen into decline. Germanic groups, such as the Franks, moved into Gaul. They brought Germanic dialects, many of which provided the roots of today's modern German language. These dialects became mixed with the Latin language spoken by the Romans.

Langue d'Oïl and Langue d'Oc

During the early Middle Ages (the ninth through the eleventh centuries), French soldiers went to fight in the Crusades. The powerful Catholic Church and the French kings were afraid of Muslim peoples invading Europe from the Middle East and North Africa. Fighting in the name of Christianity, soldiers traveled to Arab countries. Over time, the contact between

Pictured at left is a tablet inscribed with a speech given by the Roman emperor Claudius in AD 48. In the speech, which was given before the Roman Senate, Claudius requested that Gaul be allowed representation in the Senate. Pictured above is a page of a medieval French book from 1343. The text is in Latin, which was the preferred written language during the Middle Ages.

Europeans and Arabs resulted in certain Persian and Arabic words being adopted by the Romance languages.

From these mixtures, two new languages emerged: Langue d'Oïl and Langue d'Oc. Langue d'Oc (the language of Oc) was spoken in the south of France. Langue d'Oïl (the language of Oil) was spoken in the north of France. Langue d'Oïl was the language used in Paris and the surrounding Île-de-France province. Since this was the region of the French capital and the royal court, over time, Langue d'Oïl became the most popular and prestigious of all the French dialects. By the fourteenth century, it had grown more important than Latin and had become the national language. This was later known as ancien français (ancient French). By then, songs and poetry were sung and spoken in Langue d'Oïl, and books were printed in the language.

The Language of Diplomacy

In 1634, King Louis XIII's minister, Cardinal Richelieu, created the Académie Française, or French Academy. Members of the academy were to set down rules and guidelines that would govern proper spoken and written French. The academy was also in charge of writing the first dictionary of the French language. Compiled by some of the leading writers of the day, the dictionary established which words were French and how they were to be spelled and pronounced. By this time, *ancien français* had evolved into *français moderne,* or modern French. For the most part, this is the official French language that is still written and spoken.

Under Louis XIII and Louis XIV, France became the most powerful nation in Europe. As a result, French grew to be the most influential European language. Foreign kings and courts, nobles, and aristocrats all took pride in speaking fluent French.

This full-length portrait of Cardinal Richelieu, founder of the Académie Française, shows him sitting at a desk next to his writing materials. This painting was done by Phillippe de Champaigne in 1636. Champaigne was a professor of the French Academy of Painting, which was founded by Louis XIV.

The Académie Française is still the official authority on the French language. Forty language authorities are appointed to serve on a council for life. Known as the immortals, they are in charge of writing French dictionaries. The most current volume was released in 2000.

It was considered a language of refined culture as well as the language of diplomacy, which was spoken by ambassadors and businessmen. Educated ladies and gentlemen learned how to read and write in French. In fact, up until the mid-twentieth century, internationally French was the most widely spoken second language. Only after World War II did English begin to take its place.

Regional Dialects

Since its earliest days as a nation, many regional languages and dialects have been spoken throughout France. Influenced by Germanic dialects, Alsatian has long been spoken in the Alsace region that lies near the German border. In the Atlantic province of Brittany, the Celtic language evolved into Breton. Corsican is spoken by residents of the Mediterranean island of Corsica, which is located between the coasts of France and Italy.

In the Basque region, which spills over from France into Spain along the Atlantic coast, residents speak their own language. The Basque language, Euskara, is unlike any other European language. Meanwhile, in the region of Catalonia, located

A young child reads a book written in the Basque language, Euskara. The origins of Euskara are unknown. The language borrows words from French, Latin, and Spanish. Today, approximately 580,000 people speak the Basque language throughout southwest France and northern Spain.

Billboards in the Ivory Coast (Côte d'Ivoire) advertise products in French. The Ivory Coast, a West African country, became a colony of France in 1893 and was forced to adopt the French language. After it gained its independence in 1960, it continued to keep French as the national language.

between the Mediterranean coast that divides France and Spain, the official language, Catalan, is a dialect of Langue d'Oc.

Langue d'Oc itself—or Occitan—is still spoken by approximately 4 million people in parts of central and southern France. In the northern regions (and ancient French provinces) of Vendée, Normandy, Lorraine, and Picardy, locals still speak Vendéen, Norman, Lorrain, and Picard. All of these dialects are based on Langue d'Oïl.

For centuries, these local languages and dialects were the main languages spoken in individual regions. However, as the power of the royal court in Paris grew, the kings tried to increase their influence by banning these dialects. After the French Revolution, there was a strong movement to unite the nation by forcing one single French language on all citizens. The result was that regional dialects were banned. Merely speaking or writing them could lead to punishment. Fortunately, since many customs, folktales, spoken expressions, and songs existed in these languages, all managed to survive.

Since World War II, a respect for the past and new political programs have placed more value on regional cultures and traditions. The ancient languages that were formerly banned are now celebrated and even taught in public schools. In the case of the Basque regions, Catalonia, and Corsica, these languages are proudly spoken by regional movements demanding more political independence and even separation from the rest of France.

French Today

To this day, the French take great pride in their language. They consider it an important part of their culture and national identity. Unsurprisingly, the most popular program on French television is the national *dictée* or spelling bee. Every year, millions of viewers tune in to watch the nail-biting finals in which contestants try to spell impossibly complicated words.

Currently, French is spoken in close to sixty countries around the world by an estimated 200 million people. These countries—ranging from Belgium, Luxembourg, Switzerland, and Canada (Québec) to many nations of central and west Africa, the Caribbean, and the South Pacific—are known as the nations of Francophonie. They share cultural, economic, and political ties based on their common use of the French language.

While concerned with promoting the French language around the world, France is also constantly involved with preserving French at home. With the increasing popularity of English as a language of business, science, and communications, the French government has cracked down against the invasion of American culture and English expressions. Strict laws exist that limit the amount of non-French music that can be played on the radio or non-French programs that can be aired on television. Advertisements and the media cannot feature English or other foreign words when there is a French equivalent.

It is the Académie Française's job to keep track of new English words being used by people and to create new French words with the same meaning. These words, such as *balladeur* for "walkman" and *logiciel* for "software," become official when they are published in the academy's dictionary, which is updated every few years.

A popular French children's book hero Petit Nicolas (Little Nicholas) has a nightmare about missing school. The cartoon is part of a story, *On a Bien Rigolé* (A Good Laugh), from the trilogy of *Le Petit Nicholas* by Jean-Jacques Sempé and René Goscinny. Petit Nicolas is a curious but often naïve boy whose seemingly ordinary daily adventures take a turn for the hilarious with the help of his school friends. Goscinny is also the author of the popular French comic book hero Astérix.

FRENCH MYTHS AND LEGENDS

4

Throughout French history, numerous folktales and legends have been told and written down. Some of the most famous of these are not only great stories with fantastic characters, but tales that have become an important part of French culture.

Medieval Legends

French literature came into being during the Middle Ages. Some of the earliest French legends were Celtic and Breton folktales. These were stories of courtly love featuring brave knights who would perform heroic deeds in order to win the hands of fair ladies.

Many of these tales took place at the mythical court of King Arthur. They featured the adventures of one of Arthur's most courageous knights, Lancelot, and his lover, Guinevere, who was King Arthur's queen. The great medieval French poet Chrétien de Troyes wrote one of the most famous versions of this romance in his book *Lancelot*.

At left is a page from *Le Roman de Lancelot du Lac*, a French telling of the Arthurian legends. The center illustration depicts Guinevere and Arthur receiving a magic chessboard. The book was written in the early fourteenth century in northern France. While some scholars believe that the first collection of Arthurian legends came from England, some believe that the legends originated in Brittany as tales told by traveling bards and minstrels. Another famous and unarguably French tale is the story "Little Red Riding Hood" by Charles Perrault. Pictured above is the illustration *Little Red Riding Hood and the Wolf*, which appeared in *Les Contes de Perrault* in 1862.

This elaborate page from a late-fifteenth-century French book depicts several scenes from the story of King Arthur: King Arthur *(top left)*, Lancelot and Guinevere *(top right)*, Sir Galahad *(bottom left)*, and the Knights of the Round Table *(bottom right)*.

Equally famous was the tale of Tristan and Iseult. This tale was recited again and again by trouvères and troubadors. These were medieval poets and musicians who traveled throughout the country telling stories. Tristan and Iseult probably originated in Brittany. But it was first written down in book form by a twelfth-century poet named Béroul under the title *Le Roman de Tristan*.

Fables of Jean de La Fontaine

In 1668, at the age of forty-seven, Jean de La Fontaine published his first book of fables. The collection was an instant success throughout France and all of Europe. La Fontaine's short tales were based on Aesop's fables as well as traditional Hindu and Persian folktales featuring animal characters. Each seemingly simple fable included a moral or lesson and was full of humorous criticisms of various human flaws such as vanity and pride.

Although this first book was dedicated to King Louis XIV's seven-year-old son, many recognized that the fables indirectly poked fun at the king's court and his subjects. In the fables, Louis XIV was often represented as the king lion or as a bull.

One of the best known of La Fontaine's fables is "The Hare and the Tortoise," in which a speedy hare challenges a slow tortoise to a race. The hare is so sure he will win

The Story of Tristan and Iseult

Tristan is the brave and handsome nephew of Marc, the king of Cornwall. After killing an evil giant, a brother of the king of Ireland, he is sent by his uncle Marc to bring back Iseult, the golden-haired daughter of the Irish king. Iseult's father agrees to let her marry Marc after Tristan kills an evil dragon. However, on the way back to Cornwall, both Tristan and Iseult mistakenly drink a magic love potion. The potion was meant to make Iseult and Marc fall in love. Instead, it works on Iseult and Tristan.

Back in Cornwall, Marc and Iseult are married, but Tristan and Iseult can't stay away from each other. After Marc discovers their love, a shameful Tristan escapes to Brittany, where he gets married. Soon after, he is wounded in battle by a poison-tipped sword. The only one who can save him from dying is Iseult. Tristan asks a messenger to send for her by boat. If the boat returns flying a white sail, Tristan will know that Iseult is on it. But if the sail is black, it means that Iseult has refused to see Tristan.

Desperate to save her true love, Iseult jumps on the boat headed for Brittany. The messenger raises a white sail. However, Tristan who is in bed, close to dying, can't see it. Furious that Iseult is coming, his jealous wife lies and tells Tristan the sail is black. Tristan is so heartbroken, he dies. When Iseult finds him dead, she dies of grief beside him.

After they are buried, side by side, a tree springs up under each lover's tomb. As it grows, the tree's branches join together. When chopped down, they always grow back together, a symbol of eternal love.

This color engraving was made by Gaston Gelibert (1850–1931) for a nineteenth-century reprinting of "The Hare and the Tortoise." Gelibert illustrated many children's books and fairy tales.

that he stops to rest in the middle of the race. The tortoise doesn't rest at all and slowly but surely wins the race due to hard work and determination.

By the time he died in 1695, La Fontaine had published 238 fables. He had become one of the most widely read French poets of all time.

Charles Perrault

Another famous seventeenth-century writer was Charles Perrault. A wealthy Parisian who was a member of the Académie Française, Perrault was responsible for inventing what was at the time a brand-new type of literature: the fairy tale. His *Stories or Tales from Times Past, with Morals: Tales of Mother Goose* (1697) was a thin volume of eight stories that became classics of world literature. His most famous fairy tales include "Cinderella," "Sleeping Beauty," "Bluebeard," "Puss in Boots," and "Mother Goose."

One of Perrault's most widely read tales is "Little Red Riding Hood." It tells the story of a little girl dressed in a red hood who goes to visit her grandmother at her cottage in the forest. On her way, she runs into a big bad wolf. The scary (and hungry) wolf hurries ahead of Little Red Riding Hood to her grandmother's cottage. After eating up the old

A title page for Jean de La Fontaine's *Fables* displays many of the animal characters gathered together.

woman, the wolf dresses up in her clothes and waits for Little Red Riding Hood. When she arrives and comments upon what an unusually large mouth her grandmother has, the disguised wolf responds, "The better to eat you with, my dear," and proceeds to swallow her up.

Obelix

Astérix and Obelix

In 1827, the world's first comic book was invented. *M. Vieux Bois* was written in French by a Swiss man named Roland Toppfer. From that time on, comic books have become a French passion and art form. They are read and adored by children and adults alike.

One of the most popular French comics of all times is a series of adventures about a group of Gauls in 50 BC, who constantly outsmart the Romans who try to conquer them. The main heroes of these stories are a tiny but crafty warrior named Astérix and his dim-witted, faithful, and gigantic friend Obelix. In each adventure, both go on missions in order to help save their village—the only Gaul settlement not yet invaded by Romans.

Created in 1959 by Albert Uderzo and René Goscinny, the *Astérix* comic books and characters are adored by the French, who see the Gauls as ancestral symbols of themselves—ready to defend French culture and lifestyle at any cost. In fact, Astérix and his companions have become so popular that they have inspired a series of films and a Disneyland-like amusement park outside of Paris.

Whenever he gets into a tight spot, Astérix relies on a magic potion that gives him superhuman strength. The secret potion is made by the village druid named Getafix. While humorous, the well-known and popular *Astérix* books feature plenty of historical details concerning Gaul and Roman culture. Everything from Roman slavery to Gallic recipes for boar are included.

Astérix

FRENCH FESTIVALS AND CEREMONIES OF ANTIQUITY AND TODAY

5

By tradition, France is a Catholic country. Although 82 percent (roughly 47 million people) of the population considers themselves Catholic, most French are not very religious. In general, church attendance is quite low compared to other Catholic countries. Nonetheless, centuries of religious traditions have been incorporated into daily French life in the form of holidays and celebrations in which all citizens participate.

Religious Holidays and Celebrations

In February or March, the feast of Mardi Gras (Fat Tuesday) is celebrated in many towns with a giant street carnival. People dressed in elaborate costumes parade through city streets amid many fancy dress balls and other parties. The most lively carnivals take place in the Mediterranean cities along the Côte d'Azur, particularly in Nice.

Mardi Gras is followed by Easter, or Pâques, which is celebrated by processions in many towns. Accompanied by church music, Catholics carrying lit torches solemnly parade through the streets, in memory of the death of Christ.

Each year, during nine days at the end of July, Bretons celebrate their culture at the Festival de Cornouaille in Quimper. The festival draws more than 250,000 people. Pictured at left are two children in traditional Breton dress. Like many countries in Europe, France celebrates Victory in Europe Day (VE Day) on May 8. The day recognizes the Nazi defeat and the end of World War II. Above, happy Parisians march in front of the Arc de Triomphe after the city of Paris is liberated by the Allies and the Free French, a military group led by Charles de Gaulle.

On April 21, 2000, many Catholics join in a Good Friday parade. Good Friday marks the death of Jesus Christ. This takes place two days prior to Easter Sunday, which marks the resurrection of Christ.

The Fête des Rois (Feast of Kings), which is also known as Little Christmas, takes place on January 6. This festival honors the three kings who brought gifts to the infant Jesus. Throughout France, families and groups of friends buy almond cakes known as galettes des rois (kings' cakes), which they eat with fizzy apple cider. Inside each cake is a small fève (bean), usually a figure made of china or plastic. Whoever finds the fève in his or her galette is crowned king or queen and must wear the cardboard crown that accompanies the cakes.

Christmas—which originated in the Middle East and celebrates the birth of Jesus Christ—was brought to France by the Romans. The first French Christmas was celebrated in the city of Reims in 496, on the day King Clovis and 3,000 of his warriors were baptized. Since then, Christmas (called Noël in French) has become one of the most popular French holidays.

On December 24, friends and families get together for a gigantic dinner with many courses. Dinner usually begins with raw oysters and foie gras (goose liver) pâté. Dessert is the traditional bûche de Noël, or Christmas log; this is a chocolate-frosted

Fête Nationale, or Bastille Day, is celebrated every July 14 in observance of the birth of the first new republic. It is celebrated with fireworks displays, parades, and parties. At right, French alpha jets leave vapor trails of blue, white, and red (the colors of the French flag) over a parade marching down the Champs-Elysées.

cake made to look like an actual log. Much wine and champagne is drunk. Dinner usually lasts until midnight, at which point many families go to midnight Mass held at a local church. The morning of December 25 (an official holiday) is for opening presents. Afterward, friends and families once again get together for a gigantic lunch with many courses, which often goes on well into the evening.

National Holidays and Celebrations

Other holidays mark meaningful dates in French history. The most important of these is July 14, which is Bastille Day. The date marks the storming of the Bastille prison and the beginning of the French Revolution, which led to the fall of the monarchy and the birth of an independent, democratic nation.

In every French city and village, Bastille Day is celebrated with military parades, bands, bonfires, and fireworks displays. The national anthem, "La Marseillaise," is played, and buildings are decorated in the colors of the French flag—blue, white, and red. Firemen hold balls in fire stations, where people of all ages dance the night away. Naturally, the biggest Bastille Day celebration of all takes place in Paris, where there is a splendid parade down the city's famous Champs-Elysées avenue and a spectacular display of fireworks that attracts thousands.

May 8 is a holiday celebrating the end of World War II. Victory in Europe Day marks the liberation of France from Nazi forces in 1945. It is celebrated with military parades. Armistice Day, which is also celebrated with military parades, occurs on November 11. It commemorates the end of World War I.

On a joyous day in late August 1944, Parisians stand in huge crowds along the Champs-Elysées. They are cheering the passing American troops who helped liberate them from Nazi control. The troops made their way toward the Arc de Triomphe. The Nazis invaded France in May 1940, shortly after their invasion of Denmark and Norway.

Seasonal and Local Holidays and Celebrations

In France, summertime brings with it *les grands vacances,* or the "big vacations." By law, French citizens have the right to at least five weeks of paid vacation per year. This means that the French take vacationing seriously. The French love to travel, particularly within France itself. In fact, more French people have second homes than in any other country.

During the summer months, many towns and villages hold their own traditional festivals. In France, every village has its own patron saint who protects it. On the saint's day (according to the Catholic calendar), the town holds celebrations in honor of the saint. One of the most popular saints is St. Jean (St. John), whose feast day is June 24. On this date, numerous towns—St. Jean de Luz and St. Jean Pied-de-Port, for example—celebrate with special foods, dancing, music, and fireworks.

A proud Frenchman from Valreas, a small town in the Rhône-Alps, wears the clothing and armor of a French Renaissance soldier. French villagers are very much in tune with the history of their regions. Before 1790, French regions were called provinces and were ruled by dukes or other royal governors who answered to the king.

Farmers prepare for the grape harvest during the Fête des Vendanges. The holiday celebrates the end of the harvest and is a way for farm owners to thank and reward their workers.

Autumn is the harvest season. In France's many wine-growing regions, this is the time in which grapes are collected and made into wine. Grape harvesting, known as the *vendanges*, is a period of hard work that brings communities together. Many harvest festivals take place during October and November. These are celebrated with eating, dancing, and, of course, much drinking of wine.

Regional and Folk Holidays

Many French regions—such as Brittany, Corsica, and the Basque country—have their own unique culture and traditions, language, music, and cuisine. During the summer, in particular, many regions have festivals that celebrate these rich, often centuries-old local traditions. These can last for days and feature the best of local music, dance, food, and drink. During these festivals, people dress in traditional costumes. These range from the white loose-fitting pants and shirts, berets, and sashes worn by Basque men to the tall, lacy caps and ornate frilly dresses worn by the women of Normandy.

Musicians and dancers in traditional French dress celebrate at the Interceltic Festival. The festival was founded in 1971. It takes place during the first week in August throughout Lorient in Brittany. It was created to honor contemporary Celtic culture and brings together people of Celtic descent from Brittany, Scotland, and Ireland.

THE RELIGIONS OF FRANCE THROUGHOUT ITS HISTORY

6

S ince its beginnings as a nation, France has largely been a Catholic country. From the Middle Ages onward, the Catholic Church had a great deal of power and influence on daily life. To this day, the countryside is dotted with cathedrals, churches, abbeys, and convents that have been around for centuries.

Beginning with King Clovis, almost all of France's monarchs were (at least officially) Catholic. In fact, the power of the church and the monarchy were inseparable until the French Revolution did away with the authority of both. The First Republic declared that France was a nation that permitted and respected all forms of religious worship. In 1905, the church and state were officially separated, and France became a thoroughly secular country. In other words, religion and religious beliefs can have no influence on any form of French government.

Early Religions

France's earliest inhabitants, the Gauls, were descended from the Celtic peoples of northern and central Europe. Celts worshipped many gods, goddesses, and spirits, many of which symbolized different natural elements, such as water, forests, sky, and earth. Celtic priests and healers were called druids. Aside from leading rituals, they made medicinal potions and powders from plants and roots.

Pictured at left, a Carthusian monk takes a walk outside the Grande Chartreuse, a medieval monastery in the Chartreuse mountains, north of the city of Grenoble. These monks' daily routines have changed very little since the fourteenth century. Most of their day is spent in prayer. Pictured above is a room in the Abbey of Port Royal des Champs that once belonged to Blaise Pascal, a French mathematician and writer of the mid-seventeenth century.

In a lush forest near Chartres (a town southwest of Paris), druids collect mistletoe for ritual purposes. Druids were known as the magicians of the Celtic people.

Today, little remains of Celtic religious practice. The most common traces are the stone crosses that dot the French countryside. These are believed to mark ceremonial sites.

Early Christianity

When the Romans conquered Gaul, they brought Christianity along with them. Between the second and fourth centuries, this new religion spread throughout much of Gaul. In 496, Christianity became officially linked with the monarchy when France's first king, Clovis, was baptized along with 3,000 of his warriors. From then on, the power of the Catholic Church became increasingly inseparable from the power of the kings and the feudal lords who ruled individual regions. French citizens were forced to obey the strict rules and authority of both.

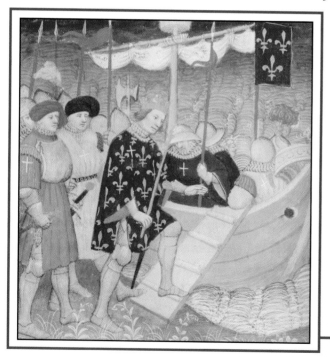

Catholicism

During the Middle Ages, new religious orders were created in France.

This fifteenth-century painting shows St. Louis leaving France to join the Crusades. St. Louis was the king of France from 1226 until 1270.

Communities of Cluniac, Benedictine, Dominican, and Franciscan monks lived in stone abbeys and monasteries that they built in the growing number of French cities and villages throughout the countryside. These monks started the first schools and universities, and they wandered around the country preaching Christian beliefs.

Above is an aerial view of the Palais des Papes (Papal Palace) in Avignon. The palace has been the home of seven popes throughout history: Pope Clement V, Pope John XXII, Pope Benedict XII, Pope Clement VI, Pope Innocent VI, Pope Urban V, and Pope Gregory XI. The town of Avignon was a papally owned property until 1791, when it was restored to France after the French Revolution.

Over time, French culture, education, and values became based on these Christian teachings and views of the world. The Catholic Church grew increasingly powerful in society. Church officials even had authority over people's souls—they would decide who would go to heaven and who would go to hell. Thanks to the generous gifts of kings and noblemen, these officials became incredibly rich. They hoped that their generosity would pardon their sins and buy them a happy afterlife. Much of this wealth can be seen in the rich interiors and treasures that still exist in France's many churches.

During the Middle Ages, many Christian pilgrims traveled across Europe to the holy city of Jerusalem. In the eleventh century, the invasion of Jerusalem by Muslims angered the Catholic pope. In 1095, Pope Urban II went to the French city of Clermont and called on all French Christians to become soldiers of the church. He urged them to pin red crosses to their chests and march to the Middle East to fight the Muslims. This first religious battle, which took place between 1096 and 1099, was known as the First Crusade ("crusade" comes from the Latin word for cross: *crux*). Over the next few centuries, there would be several Crusades, with Christian soldiers from France and other Catholic nations journeying to the Middle East.

By the 1300s, however, the people and even the French kings were angered by the corrupt practices of the increasingly powerful church, which was headed by the pope in Rome. A feud between King Philip IV and Pope Boniface VIII led to the crowning of a new French pope in the southern French city of Avignon. A magnificent papal palace was built there, from which the popes reigned until their final return to Rome in 1378.

By the 1400s, however, the power of the Catholic Church was weakening. A massive reform of its rules and authority made it less influential and opened the door to the rise of Protestantism. The reform movement preached a return to more traditional Christian values.

In the seventeenth century, however, there was a Catholic backlash against the Reformists. The Jesuit order—a very rigid Catholic order of monks—expanded enormously. It traveled to France's overseas colonies with the mission of converting and educating native peoples. Meanwhile, in France, it opened many colleges in which a strict Catholic education was given to young French people.

The monarchy itself also became strongly linked to Catholicism. Louis XIII and his powerful minister Cardinal Richelieu created the idea of an absolute, divine monarch whose power and glory came directly from God. Louis

Nuns study spiritual texts and hymns in a convent in France. Today, Catholicism is still the most widely practiced religion in France. Eighty-one percent of France's population claims to be Catholic.

XIV, the Sun King, took this idea even further, making himself the highest representative of the French Catholic Church and the highest authority of (divine) justice.

This painting, titled *The Altar of the Last Judgement*, depicts the Second Coming of Christ and the Apocalypse. It was created in 1434 by Flemish artist Roger van der Weyden.

Not surprisingly, in 1789, when the French Revolution broke out, the French masses rebelled against the authority of the kings and of the Catholic Church. Since the sixteenth century, French critics and philosophers had criticized the power of the church, arguing that all religions should be tolerated. They created the important concept of laicism. This is the idea that a government should rule its citizens without the influence of any religious authorities or beliefs. Supporters of laicism argued for a separation of the state (government) and the church. The French Revolution resulted in the creation of a French state—the First Republic—that was no longer Catholic. But it wasn't until 1905 that church and state were separated by law.

Protestantism

In the 1500s, there was a movement in France to reform the Catholic Church. Many people were angered by what they saw as an abuse of religious power. They wanted a return to a more traditional, simple Christian faith. The reform movement was led by a Frenchman named John Calvin. In 1550, he created a new church where French Protestants, known as Huguenots, could worship.

As a result, the Catholic Church thought Huguenots were traitors and criminals who were betraying the beliefs of the true French (Catholic) church. Conflicts between

This 1572 painting by the French artist François Dubois is called *Saint Bartholomew's Day Massacre.* It shows the horrifying mass killing of the Huguenots.

Catholics and Protestants erupted and eventually led to the Wars of Religion. Between 1562 and 1598, various armed conflicts between the two groups created deep divisions in the French population. The worst event occurred on the night of August 23, 1572, in Paris. Thousands of Huguenots were in the city for the wedding of Prince Henri of Navarre when Catherine de Medici (mother of King Charles) ordered the mass murder of thousands of Huguenots. Known as the St. Bartholomew's Day Massacre, the bloody killings spread from Paris to the countryside.

In 1589, when Henri of Navarre became king, he immediately signed the Edict of Nantes. This was a law that guaranteed religious and political rights to Huguenots. This period of religious tolerance only lasted until 1610, when Henri IV was murdered. Afterward, a campaign against Protestants led to the burning of their Bibles, homes, and churches. Things became worse in 1685, when Louis XIV canceled the Edict of Nantes. Many Huguenots fled from France to other European countries and to North America. Those who remained faced being burned at the stake.

By the time the Edict of Toleration (1787) had partially restored Huguenots' rights, there were no Protestant churches or schools left in France. Since then, little by little, Protestants have reconstructed their lives and places of worship. Today, there are approximately 1 million Protestants living in France.

This is a sixteenth-century portrait of Henri IV, the first king of the Bourbon dynasty. The Bourbons ruled from 1589 to 1795. The Bourbon dynasty was restored in 1814 after the rule of Napoléon. The dynasty lasted until 1848.

This is the remarkably well-preserved first page from the Edict of Nantes. This important document guaranteed religious and political rights to Huguenots.

Judaism

As early as the fourth century, there were Jews living in Roman Gaul. Five centuries later, there were many Jews at the court of Charlemagne. During the Middle Ages, their numbers and influence grew—much to the distress of the Catholic Church, who viewed all non-Catholics as evil nonbelievers. The growth of anti-Semitic attitudes put forth by the church led to much persecution of Jews in France. Finally, in the fourteenth century, they were expelled from France altogether.

During the Renaissance, small groups of Jews returned to France. To keep from being persecuted, some pretended to convert to Catholicism, but secretly they maintained their religious and cultural traditions. These Jews were known as New Christians.

Only after the French Revolution were Jews allowed to enjoy the full rights of French citizens. The passing of the Edict of Tolerance allowed them to openly practice their religion. Toward the end of the eighteenth century, a wave of Jewish immigrants from eastern Europe substantially increased the number of Jews in France. During the nineteenth century, Jews moved out of isolated ghettos and became an accepted part of French society. Meanwhile, they were able to keep hanging on to their religion and traditions.

While Jews participated in French political and cultural life, envy of their increased success and visibility created a new wave of discrimination. This anti-Semitism came to a head in the famous Dreyfus affair. In 1894, a French soldier named Alfred Dreyfus was falsely accused of spying simply due to the fact that he was Jewish. As punishment, he was sentenced to life imprisonment. However, many outraged citizens, including novelist Émile Zola, came to his defense. Finally, twelve years into his sentence, he was pardoned by the president.

In the twentieth century, anti-Semitism once again took hold of the country. When the Nazis invaded France during World War II, the Vichy government began

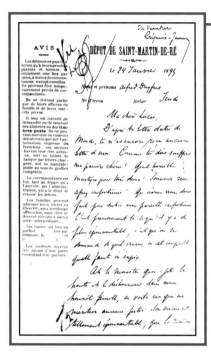

This letter was sent by Captain Alfred Dreyfus to his wife, dated January 24, 1895, to inform her of his arrest for supposed spying and his imprisonment at Devil's Island. Dreyfus was eventually pardoned on September 19, 1899.

persecuting Jews. Although some Resistance fighters helped by hiding Jews, the Nazis and their French allies succeeded in rounding up one-quarter of France's Jewish population. Then they sent them off to concentration camps, where they were killed.

In the 1950s and 1960s, France received a new wave of Jewish immigrants. This group arrived from North Africa, in particular from the former French colonies of Morocco and Algeria. Today, France—which is home to more than half a million Jews—has the fifth largest Jewish population in the world and the largest in western Europe.

Islam

Islam is the second most important religion in France. Though Muslim immigration to France is quite recent, more than 4 million people (roughly 7 percent of the population) are Muslims. At present, most Muslims living in France are either North African immigrants or their children. The majority of them come from Algeria, Morocco, and Tunisia—all of which were French colonies until the 1960s.

There were few Muslims living in France before the twentieth century. During World War I, many North African Muslims were drafted into the French army. Those who weren't killed in the war

This political cartoon depicts Alfred Dreyfus as a multi-headed snakelike creature. A sword piercing him carries the label "le Traitre" (the traitor). Because anti-Semitism was so common, many believed that Dreyfus was guilty of espionage based on the fact that he was Jewish.

On a September morning in 2000, Muslims bow toward Mecca as they pray during a protest in Nice. The protest took place in response to Nice mayor Jacques Peyrat's refusal to permit the construction of a mosque in the town.

settled in France. In 1920, construction began on Paris's Grand Mosque, a magnificent building that to this day is the most important Islamic center of worship and culture in the country.

During World War II, more North African Muslims fought alongside French soldiers before settling down in France. Then, in the 1960s and early 1970s, France experienced an economic boom so great that there weren't enough workers. Thousands of North Africans were hired for difficult manual and factory jobs. Most of these jobs paid such low wages that few French workers would accept them. Generous immigration laws allowed North African workers and their families to settle in France. By the early 1980s, there were suddenly more than 2 million Muslims living in major French cities.

Unfortunately, this increase in the Muslim population led to a rise in anti-Islamic sentiment. Also, the popularity of the right-wing National Front Party increased. Its leader, Jean-Marie Le Pen, warned that French culture was being threatened by immigrants, specifically Muslims, who had different religious beliefs. Such warnings scared some French citizens. Another concern was the growing number of poor, unemployed, and angry young Muslims. Forced to live in the outskirts of French cities, they often clashed with police. As a result, the French government cracked down on immigration. They rounded up many illegal immigrants and sent them back to North Africa.

Today, France has six major mosques and more than 1,000 small mosques where Muslims worship. Although many Muslims feel integrated into French society, others encounter racial conflicts. For example, the Muslim traditions of having more than one wife and of girls and women wearing head scarves at all times have created cultural clashes in a society that wants to hang on to its "Frenchness" and stay true to its tradition of laicism.

THE ART AND ARCHITECTURE OF FRANCE

S ince the Middle Ages, France has been one of the world's major artistic centers. The Catholic Church, kings, and democratically elected governments always viewed the arts as an extremely important part of French culture. For centuries, Paris has attracted artists from around the globe, making the French capital one of the world's most exciting and creative cities. At the same time, the richness and influence of French art has been felt all over the world.

Early Art

The earliest known examples of art in France are cave paintings that date back to Paleolithic times (between 10,000 and 30,000 years ago). These paintings decorated the walls of many caverns in southwest France. The most famous are the paintings at the caves of Lascaux. Featuring sticklike people and animals such as bulls and deer, these paintings were the works of the Cro-Magnon peoples.

When the Romans occupied Gaul, they brought along many elements of their sophisticated civilization. They built and settled numerous trading towns, especially along the Mediterranean coast. Cities such as Marseilles, Nice, and Arles were all founded by

Pictured at left is the famous *Icarus,* from a series of works by Henri Matisse called Jazz. Matisse painted in the fauvist style and was mostly influenced by the works of Paul Cézanne, Paul Gauguin, and Édouard Manet. Pictured above is the Richelieu wing of the Louvre museum. The Louvre has one of the best collections of art in the world. It is home to such well-renowned works as Leonardo da Vinci's *Mona Lisa*.

Some of the earliest-known art can be found in the Lascaux caves in Dordogne, France. This rock painting, depicting a leaping cow and several small horses, is approximately 15,000 years old.

Romans, who constructed theaters, palaces, fountains, and temples—some of which still exist.

The first examples of French art and architecture began to emerge with the fall of the Roman Empire. With the spread of Christianity, many abbeys and monasteries were built to house religious orders of nuns and monks. In the eighth century, there was a great surge in the construction of churches. These were ornately decorated with painted murals, mosaics, sculpted gold, and tapestries.

Middle Ages

The growth of cities coupled with the desire of the Catholic Church, French kings, and nobles to show off their wealth gave birth to an architectural style known as French Gothic. Between the twelfth and sixteenth centuries, monstrous Gothic cathedrals sprang up in major French cities.

The Gothic craze began in the north, where there was

This is an aerial view of a second-century Roman amphitheater in Arles, France. During the Roman Empire, Arles was an important city. At one point in the fifth century, it was declared the capital of the west by Emperor Constantine III.

Notre-Dame de Paris (Our Lady of Paris) is located on the Île de la Cité in the center of Paris. Construction of the great cathedral began in 1163 and ended nearly 200 years later in 1345. Throughout its history, many royal ceremonies have been held at Notre-Dame, including the coronation of Napoléon in 1804.

an abundance of good building stone that was easy to carve. It then spread to the south and the rest of Europe. Gothic buildings, particularly cathedrals, soared to great heights. They were supported by external vaults called flying buttresses and were illuminated by brilliant "roses" or wheel-shaped windows made of stained glass. Both interiors and exteriors were decorated with figures such as angels, saints, kings, and demonic monsters called gargoyles. Sculpted out of stone, the gargoyles were incredibly lifelike.

The first and most famous of the Gothic churches was the Abbey of St. Denis, built in 1140 on the outskirts of Paris. This royal church was the burial place for all the kings of France. Other magnificent examples of Gothic architecture are the Notre-Dame de Paris, and the cathedrals of Chartres, Reims, and Amiens. Many of their interiors feature painted panels of scenes from the Bible. This is because, at the time, most paintings in France were of religious subjects.

Renaissance and Baroque

In the beginning of the sixteenth century, the new style of the Italian Renaissance began to influence French art and architecture. In the early 1500s, King François I invited several leading artists (including the legendary Leonardo da Vinci) to carry out works in France. Soon, all the châteaux of kings and nobles around Paris and the Loire Valley were being built in the new style with high roofs and grand exteriors that resembled the monumental buildings of ancient Rome and Greece. In the Loire Valley, the most famous châteaux were those of Blois, Chambord, Chenonceau, and Fontainebleau. Their interiors were filled with ornate ballrooms and galleries that were decorated by a group of Italian artists who had settled in Fontainebleau.

This intricate and breathtaking stained-glass window is from the north wall of Chartres Cathedral. The cathedral, built in the thirteenth century, remains one of the last great examples of the Gothic style.

French art of the seventeenth century was also heavily influenced by Italian art. The ornate baroque style popular in Italy was imported to France and adapted to the great projects of Louis XIII and Louis XIV. During the late 1600s, Louis XIV built impressive monuments to French glory, including his own magnificent palace at Versailles. This extravagant project was the work of leading architect Jules Hardouin-Mansart. He also designed numerous squares and public buildings in Paris.

French painting during this time also reflected what was going on in Italy. Many of France's leading painters, such as Nicolas Poussin and Claude Lorrain, worked and studied in Italy. In 1663, the French Academy of Painting and Sculpture came into being. The academy's artists were paid by the court of Louis XIV to create artworks that showed the glory of the Sun King. Painters created panels, tapestries, and murals that likened the king to famous heroes from classical literature. Meanwhile, sculptors created enormous statues of the king in heroic poses that would decorate France's public squares and gardens.

Eighteenth-Century Art and Architecture

The first part of the eighteenth century witnessed a reaction against the grandeur of Louis XIV and the court of Versailles. With the death of the Sun King, the influence of the court at Versailles declined. Many aristocrats and wealthy merchants moved to the center of Paris, where they entertained in elegant mansions called *hôtels particuliers*. These homes were decorated with elegant art and furnishings in the highly ornamental rococo style. Rococo is characterized by natural shapes and a lot of delicate detail.

Painting and sculpture were also less grandiose. Leaving behind serious subjects such as battles and aristocratic portraits, leading artists painted people in contemporary clothing enjoying themselves at picnics and parties. Antoine Watteau

This is an aerial view of the Château de Chambord. It was built between 1519 and 1539. King François I intended the château to be a huge hunting lodge. He hoped this would give his enemies the impression that he was very rich. The château has 6 towers, 440 rooms, 84 staircases, and 365 fireplaces. It is the largest château in the Loire Valley.

used striking colors to paint pictures of couples strolling in soft, dreamy landscapes. François Boucher and Jean-Honoré Fragonard also used rich colors to paint scenes of rosy-cheeked, sensual women in alluring poses. These artists and their subject matter were popular with Louis XV and Louis XVI, both of whom enjoyed the carefree, pleasure-seeking Parisian arts scene.

At the end of the French monarchy and the French Revolution, such art was seen as silly and unimportant. The end of the eighteenth century brought with it the First Republic and the rise of Napoléon. These political changes were accompanied by a return to subjects that celebrated the glory of France. The leading painter of this period was Jacques-Louis David. His paintings celebrated republican ideals of liberty and democracy, as well as scenes from contemporary history. Most famous of these are his portraits of Napoléon and *Death of Marat* (1793), which shows the revolutionary Jean-Paul Marat stabbed to death in his bath.

In architecture, this return to grand forms resulted in the neoclassical style. Buildings were modeled after the monumental architecture of ancient Greece

This painting, *Shepherdess Seated with Sheep and a Basket of Flowers near a Ruin in a Wooded Landscape,* was created by French rococo artist Jean-Honoré Fragonard. Fragonard's paintings are characteristically light and often depict playful scenes.

and Rome. Such architecture was very simple, with little decoration.

The Nineteenth Century

In the late 1700s to mid-1900s, France became caught up in the romantic movement. Romantic artists valued emotions over everything else. They were also fascinated with nature and change. In France, three great romantic painters emerged during this period. Théodore Géricault explored intense human emotions in works such as *Raft of the Medusa* (1818), which depicts the horror of shipwreck victims. Jean-Auguste-Dominique Ingres reflected the French romantics' fascination with sensual and exotic subjects. He painted many female nudes in foreign settings, the most famous of which is *The Great Odalisque* (1814). Meanwhile, Eugène Delacroix used strong brushstrokes and bright colors in his paintings of female nudes and dramatic scenes that were inspired by historical events. One of the best known is his *Liberty Guiding the People* (1830), painted to celebrate the Revolution of 1830.

By the mid-1800s, the strong emotions of romanticism had given way to the true-to-life subjects of realism. Leading realist painter Gustave Courbet thought that an artist's job was to paint scenes from daily life. Courbet's paintings of peasants, such as *Funeral at Ornans* (1850), caused a scandal when they were viewed. It was the first time ordinary people had been the subjects of a painting. Because of their subject matter, Courbet's paintings were seen as ugly and improper. Painter Jean-François Millet was also interested in the lives of ordinary French farmers and workers. His most famous work, *The Gleaners* (1857), shows peasants working in a field.

Claude Monet painted *Water Lilies*. Monet was fond of painting the nature that flourished in his own backyard, particularly the water lilies in his pond. Monet's garden is called Giverny and is open to the public.

The nineteenth century also saw the rise of landscape painting. The invention of tubes of mixed paint meant that, for the first time, artists could do plein air (outdoor) painting. One of the great natural landscape painters of the nineteenth century was Camille Corot.

Another painter who explored new and, at the time, scandalous subjects was Édouard Manet. Manet wasn't interested in paintings that taught a lesson or showed "proper subjects." He believed in "art for art's sake," which was a revolutionary idea at the time. So were his original paintings of scenes from Paris's bars and public places, which, like his famous *Luncheon on the Grass* (1863), were painted in bold, contrasting colors. Equally colorful and lively were the paintings of dancers, prostitutes, actresses, and barmaids painted by Henri de Toulouse-Lautrec. Toulouse-Lautrec captured the festive atmosphere of bohemian Paris in the hilly neighborhood of Montmartre. He even lived in a brothel for some time while he painted pictures of prostitutes.

In the 1870s, Manet began to paint outdoors. His plein air paintings were greatly admired by a new group of painters known as the impressionists. The impressionists saw their subjects in terms of patches of light and color.

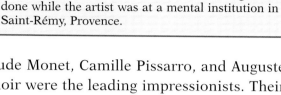

This 1889 self-portrait of Vincent van Gogh was done while the artist was at a mental institution in Saint-Rémy, Provence.

Claude Monet, Camille Pissarro, and Auguste Renoir were the leading impressionists. Their paintings mostly featured seacoasts and riverbanks. In these locations, light was reflected in many different ways, depending on the time of day. Monet's studies of how light changes objects were especially detailed. This is evident in his series of paintings, *Poplars* (1891) and *Water Lilies* (1899–1926).

Another great painter of the time was Edgar Degas. Degas was less concerned with light than with movement. His paintings and sculptures of ballerinas and circus performers brilliantly captured figures in motion.

Four nineteenth-century painters would have a particularly great influence on twentieth-century modern art: Georges Seurat, Paul Cézanne, Paul Gauguin, and Vincent van Gogh. Like the impressionists, Seurat was fascinated with theories about light and color. His paintings were made up of thousands of tiny pinpricks of color that a viewer could only detect when up close. Cézanne saw objects as geometric shapes. In his paintings, he broke down his subject matter (whether landscapes, swimmers, or bowls of fruit) into basic forms such as cubes, cylinders, and triangles.

Paul Gauguin poses in front of one of his paintings at his home in France. Gauguin's experimental style eventually inspired twentieth-century fauvist artists such as Matisse.

Auguste Rodin's massive sculpture of the French novelist Honoré de Balzac stands in a garden outside of the Rodin Museum in Paris. Today it is one of the most recognized statues in the world.

Gauguin was a wealthy banker who retired at thirty-five to paint full-time. Influenced by Japanese prints and stained glass, he created works in which large slabs of unusually bright colors suggested primitive emotions. In later life, Gauguin moved to Tahiti, where he painted his most famous works. Gauguin had a complicated friendship with van Gogh. Of Dutch origin, the depressed but brilliant painter slapped great slabs of paint directly onto the canvas. The textured surfaces and energetic brushstrokes revealed van Gogh's intense emotions, particularly in his late paintings such as *Wheatfield with Crows* (1890).

The nineteenth century also saw many other revolutions in terms of the arts. Auguste Rodin sculpted incredibly lifelike male and female nudes, whose every gesture was full of emotion. In terms of architecture, buildings of the 1800s alternated between the traditional neo-classical style and a more luxurious neobaroque style (an example of which is Charles Garnier's spectacular Paris Opera House). By the 1880s, new advances in industrial materials and engineering led to some fantastic experiments, most notably the famous Eiffel Tower. Designed by the

engineer Gustave Eiffel, it has become a symbol of Paris and one of the best-known landmarks in the world.

Twentieth-Century Art

The twentieth century got off to a colorful start with the fauvist exhibition of 1905, in Paris. *Fauves* is French for "wild beasts." However, the term was given to a group of artists including Henri Matisse, André Derain, and Georges Rouault, whose paintings used wild colors that had no relation to the objects they painted (imagine bright green skies and hot-pink seas). Fauvism was the first of many radical movements that brought artists from all over Europe to Paris to take part in the exciting new artistic experiments occurring there.

One of the most famous newcomers was the Spanish-born painter Pablo Picasso. Although he had many different phases as a painter, Picasso's great invention was cubism. Together with Georges Braque, Picasso painted everyday objects such as bottles, tables, and guitars from various angles. The confusing but revolutionary result—objects cut up into numerous angles, pieces, and cubes—marked the beginning of

This 1892 painting by Paul Gauguin is called *Two Women in Idyllic Scenery with Orange Dog*. Gauguin is considered to be responsible for the start of the fauvist movement, which followed post-impressionism.

Picasso's *Les Demoiselles D'Avignon* is considered to be a forerunner of cubism. The 1907 painting depicts five prostitutes in a brothel. Their bodies are flat and abstractly drawn. Two of the figures are wearing hideous masks.

abstract art. Unlike realistic artists, who aim to copy a recognizable scene from life, abstract artists are more interested in interpreting what they see in a nonrealistic manner that often bears little or no resemblance to the subjects in question.

The horrors of World War I led many artists to reject European culture, which was seen as fake and meaningless. As a result, a group of artists called the Dadaists looked to the "primitive" art of Africa and the South Pacific and common objects that were normally seen as ugly. Marcel Duchamp was one of the most radical of these artists. His "ready-made" objects (bicycle wheels and sinks, for example) challenged traditional art and values.

Another group of artists who wanted to shock and challenge traditional values were the surrealists. Their work was inspired by dreams, nightmares, the unconscious, and the works of the great psychoanalyst Sigmund Freud. The paintings of Spanish-born Salvador Dalí, German-born Max Ernst, and Yves Tanguy featured disturbing landscapes filled with melting clocks, giant ants, and other unsettling objects.

The outbreak of World War II and the German invasion of France caused many artists to leave France for New York City. After the war, the last truly French art movement was called New Realism. During the 1950s and 1960s, the most important New Realists transformed everyday objects into unusual new works. Jean Dubuffet used materials such as tar, sand, and junk to fashion enormous human sculptures. Arman and César also made giant works out of an assemblage of everyday objects, including broken lamps, telephones, and garbage. Swiss-born Jean Tinguely made fantastic moving sculptures that twirled and whirled like great machines. An important New Realist was Yves Klein. In search of pure color, Klein created a pure blue that he patented and

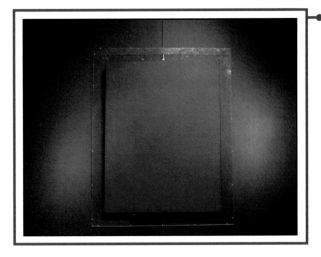

International Klein Blue is a 11-square-foot (1 sq m) square of canvas painted a unique shade of blue by French artist Yves Klein. Klein was born in Nice, France, in 1928 and died suddenly on June 6, 1962, in Paris.

called International Klein Blue. Often, he covered entire canvases and sculptures with this deep, rich blue.

Twentieth-Century Architecture

The diversity and innovations in twentieth-century French art were mirrored by those in French architecture. The beginning of the century saw the creation of the art nouveau style with its soft curves and curling organic vines and flowers. Famous examples include the early Métro (subway) stations in Paris, designed by Hector Guimard, and the elegant Parisian department stores. In the 1920s and 1930s, many apartment buildings were constructed in the sophisticated style known as art deco. Its clean lines and curves were inspired by fast cars and ocean liners.

Similar to art deco was the international style, whose greatest practitioner was the Swiss-French architect known as Le Corbusier. One of the leading architects of the twentieth century, Le Corbusier's revolutionary glass boxes—houses that he

At left is one of many art nouveau Paris Métro entrances that were designed by French architect Hector Guimard. He designed the entrances and built them out of cast iron between 1899 and 1902.

Swiss-French architect Charles Edouard Jeanneret's church, La Chapelle de Notre-Dame de Haut, is located in Ronchamp, France. Jeanneret is more commonly referred to as Le Corbusier. He is considered one of the greatest architects of the twentieth century.

built in Marseilles and Paris—marked the beginnings of modern architecture.

Like French kings before them, French presidents like to leave their mark on France by creating great monuments. In the 1970s, President Georges Pompidou commissioned the Georges Pompidou Center, a contemporary arts center in the heart of Paris. Architects Renzo Piano and Richard Rogers created a glass building in which all the electrical, heating, and water pipes are not only visible but are painted in bright colors.

In the late 1980s, President Mitterrand commissioned architect Jean Nouvel to create the Institut du Monde Arabe, a museum of Arab culture whose light-sensitive shutters open and close like eyes, depending on the amount of sunlight. At the same time, Carlos Ott designed the futuristic Bastille Opera House, and Ieoh Ming Pei built a giant glass pyramid that serves as an entrance to the Louvre museum. More recently, Dominique Perrault created the newly opened French National Library, whose spectacular four-building complex cleverly resembles four open books.

LES
PRECIEVSES
RIDICVLES.
COMEDIE

REPRESENTE'E
au Petit Bourbon.

A PARIS,

Chez GVILLAVME DE LVYNE,
Libraire-Iuré, au Palais, dans la
Salle des Merciers, à la Iustice.

M. DC. LX.
AVEC PRIVILEGE DV ROY.

THE LITERATURE AND MUSIC OF FRANCE

8

The first examples of French literature emerged in the eleventh century. *Chansons de gestes* were long poems that narrated the heroic deeds of the knights who fought alongside Charlemagne. The masterpiece of them all is the "Song of Roland" (mid-eleventh century). This poem describes the death of Charlemagne's nephew, Roland, who was attacked during a battle in the Pyrenees. It was the first work of literature to awaken a feeling of French identity and nationalism.

The Middle Ages

In the twelfth century, a new type of literature appeared. *Romans courtois* were tales of courtly love that were read aloud to kings and nobles. These stories featured knights who braved all dangers to win the hands of beautiful ladies. Many were set in the court of King Arthur and borrowed elements from Celtic mythology. The major French poet of this period was Chrétien de Troyes, author of *Lancelot* (circa 1170) and *Perceval* (circa 1185).

Outside royal courts and aristocratic circles, different kinds of stories were created to teach and entertain the masses. *Fabliaux* were simple, poetic tales that poked fun at everything from women to church officials.

Pictured at left is the title page from the first printing of Molière's *Les Précieuses Ridicules* (The Affected Young Ladies), which was written in 1660. *Les Précieuses Ridicules* is considered one of Molière's masterpieces. Above is a painting that accompanies a medieval French tale, *Roman de la Rose* (Romance of the Rose). The story tells of the journeys of a young man searching for his one true love.

Fables are tales with morals in which animal characters are used to make fun of human flaws such as pride, vanity, and selfishness.

The first works of French music also emerged during the Middle Ages. Initially, there were two types of music: religious chants and hymns. These were played and sung in Catholic churches by members of religious orders. A more popular music was performed by roving troubadours.

Renaissance

The invention of the printing press in the fifteenth century helped to popularize the works of many French writers. It was during the 1500s that François Rabelais wrote some of the greatest comic works of world literature. His multivolume stories featuring the giant Gargantua and his son Pantagruel were filled with irony and outrageous, sometimes gross, humor.

New forms also emerged in French poetry. Pierre de Ronsard, the leader of a group of poets called the Pléiade, wrote lyrical sonnets that were quite revolutionary. They freed French poetry from the traditionally serious writing style that imitated classical Greek and Latin poetry.

During the Renaissance, music was dominated by the works of Italian and Dutch composers. However, inspired by the new movements in poetry, the chanson—a light, melodic song invented in France—spread throughout Europe.

Classicism

During the seventeenth century, France's position as the most powerful nation in Europe was matched by the glory and influence of French literature. This golden age produced what is now referred to as classic French literature. Works

A poster advertising a turn-of-the-century film based on Jean Racine's *Athalie*. The poster was done by Paul Berthon and is in typical art nouveau style.

Actor Douglas Rain performs on stage as Jourdain in Molière's *Le Bourgeois Gentilhomme* at the 1964 Stratford Festival in Ontario, Canada. *Le Bourgeois Gentilhomme* was first performed in 1670 by the Troupe de Roi.

created during this time are still studied by all French schoolchildren. In 1634, Cardinal Richelieu founded the Académie Française. The academy not only preserved the French language, but it created literary rules that led to the invention of harmonious, well-balanced prose and poetry that was considered "classic."

This classical period witnessed the appearance of France's greatest playwrights. Pierre Corneille wrote more than thirty plays, including the tragic masterpiece *Le Cid* (1637). Even more popular was Jean Racine, whose simpler, more realistic and tragic plays *Andromache* (1667) and *Phaedra* (1677) revealed a world of intense passions. These plays were written in elegant rhyming verse as were the hilarious comedies of Molière. Molière's masterpieces *Tartuffe* (1664) and *Le Misanthrope* (1666) combined ridiculous farce with criticisms of personal and social issues.

The seventeenth century also saw the rise of the French novel. Up until the mid-1600s, French novels had been long-winded affairs full of hard-to-believe adventures. In 1678, the Comtesse de la Fayette published *The Princess of Clèves* (1678), a novel about the problems of a married couple. The book became a model for many future novels that were driven by complex characters instead of silly plots.

The leading form of music in the seventeenth century was opera. French composers combined elements of opera, ballet, and spoken drama/dialogue in a form known as opera-ballet. The melodies were simpler than the long, elaborate arias of Italian opera. One of the greatest composers of this period was Jean-Baptiste Lully.

This painting by Jacques Andre Joseph Camelot Aved shows the composer and musical theorist Jean-Philippe Rameau plucking a violin. Rameau wrote six operas and three ballets, as well as various instrumental works.

The Enlightenment

In the eighteenth century, France experienced many new advances in science. The decline of the power of both the church and the monarchy caused writers and philosophers to question traditional notions and institutions. Many of these "enlightened" ideas found their way into eighteenth-century literature. One of the greatest and most critical writer-philosophers of this time was Voltaire. He was most famous for philosophical tales (such as *Zadig* [1747] and *Candide* [1759]) that playfully mixed arguments about intolerance and injustice with great characters and storytelling.

Novels of the eighteenth century also became much more sophisticated. Many of the most successful, such as Abbé Prévost's *Manon Lescaut* (1731) and Pierre Choderlos de Laclos's *Dangerous Liaisons* (1782), revolved around characters that learned lessons about life through love. Love and passion were also the themes of the great playwrights of the period. For example, Beaumarchais authored *Le Barber de Séville* (1775) and *Le Marriage de Figaro* (1784).

In terms of music, the great French composer and theorist of the period was Jean-Philippe Rameau. Not only did Rameau write some of the best operas of the eighteenth century, he also wrote books about harmony in music that are still referred to today. During this period, the first French symphonies were composed. Many of the finest were the works of François-Joseph Gossec.

Romanticism

In the early nineteenth century, romantic ideas, which had become very popular in France, influenced every kind of art. Romanticism was all about a writer or artist being guided by his or her innermost passions. Romantic works were also inspired by nature.

Taken with romantic ideals, major French poets created some of the most original and passionate poetry ever. Foremost among the romantic poets were Alphonse

Palais Garnier, a neobaroque-style opera house, is one of Paris's many landmarks. It is decorated with expensive velvet, gold leaf, and several statues.

de Lamartine, author of *Meditations* (1826), Alfred de Vigny, and Alfred de Musset. But perhaps the greatest of all was Victor Hugo. Over a sixty-five-year career, he wrote bold fiction and poetry that touched on the major romantic themes. He was also the author of the famous novels *The Hunchback of Notre Dame* (1831) and *Les Misérables* (1820), both of which focused on sweeping human and social issues.

Other major novelists included Stendhal, Alexandre Dumas, and George Sand. Stendhal, author of *The Red and the Black* (1830), wrote about characters whose lives were dominated by passion. Dumas wrote historical novels that combined exciting adventure with French history. Meanwhile, George Sand wasn't really a George at all, but a woman named Aurore Dupin. An early feminist, she invented her male pseudonym in order to have her works published.

In the nineteenth century, both the Paris Conservatory and the National Opera opened. Soon after, Paris began to attract famous musicians from all over Europe, such as Frédéric Chopin and Franz Liszt. The great French composer of the romantic era was Hector Berlioz. In order to play the grandiose, sweeping melodies he composed, he expanded the number of musicians and instruments in French orchestras.

This photogravure of Victor Hugo was taken in 1870 by French photographer Goupil. Hugo was elected as an immortal to the Académie Francaise in 1841.

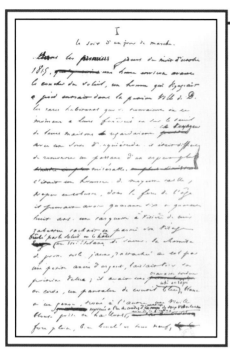

This 1862 page from Victor Hugo's famous novel *Les Miserables* shows the manuscript in Hugo's own handwriting. While Hugo is largely considered a novelist by non-French-speaking readers, he actually wrote much more poetry.

Realism

Around the middle of the nineteenth century, some writers and artists rebelled against what they viewed as the overly emotional aspects of romanticism. They preferred themes that reflected social problems in a more objective, journalistic manner. Honoré de Balzac created a series of novels that, together, made up what he called the *Human Comedy* (1842–1848). As a whole, the *Human Comedy* featured more than 2,000 characters. Writers and prostitutes, farmers and countesses—all were described with rich detail. The novels offer an incredibly true-to-life description of nineteenth-century French society.

Other great writers included Gustave Flaubert, Guy de Maupassant, and Émile Zola. Flaubert's *Madame Bovary* (1857) tells the bleak story of a bored country wife who has a tragic love affair. Maupassant's specialty was brilliant short stories, filled with realistic details and plenty of ironic humor. Meanwhile, like Balzac before him, Émile Zola created a series of twenty novels that examine every aspect of French social life. Because many of his subjects were often depressing, Zola's works were important examples of a new movement called naturalism, which sought to reveal the uglier aspects of French life.

The poet Charles Baudelaire was also concerned with the dark side of life. His famous book of poetry, *The Flowers of Evil* (1857), mixed depressing images with beautiful verse in an unusual way. Baudelaire's vision of the suffering poet became very influential. His work inspired many poets of his generation, including Arthur Rimbaud and Paul Verlaine. Rimbaud and Verlaine both created original, highly experimental poetry. Stéphane Mallarmé, another poet, inspired the symbolist movement with his strong images, or symbols, and musical way with words.

At the end of the nineteenth century, a return to past musical traditions inspired composers Camille Saint-Saëns and César Franck to revive French organ

This photograph of French author Honoré de Balzac was taken circa 1835 to 1845. Balzac was famous for his good work habits, which included twelve- to fifteen-hour workdays.

and church music. French operas thrived with the works of Georges Bizet and Charles Gounod. Meanwhile, the impressionist movement in art—seen in the paintings of Monet and Renoir—spilled over into music in the works of Claude Debussy and Maurice Ravel. Heavily improvised and full of "impressions," many of these works were called art songs.

Modernism

Major events of the twentieth century—industrialization, the Great Depression, and two world wars—created a French literary scene full of change and experimentation as authors and poets tackled new themes in original ways. French poets embraced the twentieth-century artistic and literary movement known as modernism. Modernism was revolutionary for its lack of rules and its exploration of new, often shocking themes. Leading French modernist poets were Paul Claudel, Paul Valéry, and Guillaume Apollinaire. Apollinaire was responsible for inventing the term "surrealist," which was later adopted by a group of writers and artists. Obsessed with dreams, nightmares, and fantasies, these surrealists wrote poems full of disturbing and surprising images that came from their deep unconscious.

Following in the tradition of Balzac and Zola, cyclical novels—a series of novels that, taken as a whole, evoked an entire universe—were very popular. In his multivolume masterpiece, *Remembrance of Things Past* (1913–1927), Marcel Proust tried to recapture past events by reconstructing (through memory) the objects and sensations that he had seen and experienced. Other major novelists, all of whom dealt with the modernist themes of man struggling against complicated social rules, included André Gide, Colette, François Mauriac, Louis-Ferdinand Céline, and André Malraux.

Existentialism

World War II and the Nazi invasion of France devastated the nation as well as French citizens' sense of identity. Unsurprisingly, doubts about life, death, and existence led to

This photograph shows Jean-Paul Sartre and Simone de Beauvoir deep in conversation at a café in Paris.

literature that revolved around themes of destruction, disease, and shattered identity.

Many such concerns were dealt with by the existentialists, a group of writers and thinkers who questioned the meaning of human life. An important existentialist was Albert Camus, author of novels *The Stranger* (1942) and *The Plague* (1947). But the leader of the movement was his friend Jean-Paul Sartre, author of the novel *Nausea* (1938) and a play *No Exit* (1944). Sartre's long-term companion, Simone de Beauvoir, was a feminist as well as an existentialist. Her book *The Second Sex* (1949) remains one of the classics of feminist thought and literature.

The French theater from the post–World War II period explored similar issues. Leading playwrights included Jean Giraudoux, author of *The Madwoman of Chaillot* (1946), and Jean Anouilh. Jean Genet, a former prison inmate, wrote hard-hitting, psychological plays such as *The Balcony* (1956) and *The Blacks* (1956). These plays tackled subjects such as destructive instincts and lives lived on the edge of society.

Meanwhile, Eugène Ionesco and Samuel Beckett created the theater of the absurd, in which sets, plot, dialogue, and character were purposely vague and meaningless—this was meant to be a reflection of modern life itself. A classic example of this style is Samuel Beckett's famous play *Waiting for Godot* (1954). The entire play revolves around two characters sitting under a tree and talking nonsense while they wait for a character, Godot, who never arrives.

Similar themes were explored in the novels of the 1950s and 1960s. In the most experimental of these novels, there was often little or no plot, characters, or dialogue. These radical experiments led to the birth of *le roman nouvel,* or the antinovel. Leading authors who sought to create works of fiction that weren't novels included Alain Robbe-Grillet, Michel Butor, and Nathalie Sarraute.

This is a cover for a book of sheet music for the song "The Charleston." The cover art was done by R. de Valerio and features Josephine Baker dancing the Charleston at the Folies-Bergères in Paris.

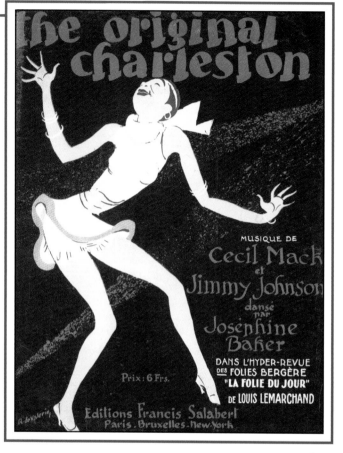

Twentieth-Century Music

French music of the twentieth century was also extremely diverse. In the early 1900s, the French chanson, or popular song, was reinvented. Crowds filled the music halls of Paris to see the shows put on by troops of dancing girls such as the Folies Bergères, as well as leading performers such as Mistinguet, Maurice Chevalier, and Josephine Baker. In the 1920s, African and Afro-American rhythms became the rage, and Paris became the capital of jazz.

The 1950s and 1960s were the era of the *grands chansonniers* (great singers). Charles Trenet, Edith Piaf, and Jacques Brel belted out heartbreaking French ballads. Meanwhile, Juliette Gréco and Jeanne Moreau sang *chansons intellectuels* (intellectual songs), whose lyrics were written by poets such as Jacques Prévert and Sartre. Although many people (both inside and outside of France) have criticized popular French music of the late twentieth century for being trivial, singer/songwriters such as Serge Gainsbourg, Jacques Higelin, Bernard Lavilliers, and Alain Souchon have mixed moving and poetic lyrics with inventive melodies.

Meanwhile, classical music of the twentieth century proved to be more direct, simple, and accessible. One of the greatest modern composers was Erik Satie. More recent composers like Olivier Messiaen are more experimental. Messiaen composed original music that borrows from other sources such as Eastern and electronic music.

FAMOUS FOODS AND RECIPES OF FRANCE

 French cooking is famous throughout the world. Recipes and cooking techniques, developed over centuries, have made French cuisine a refined art. Even the simplest dishes require careful preparation.

Regional Cooking

French cuisine is extremely varied. Dishes change from place to place, depending on the ingredients and traditions of each region. In general, there is a difference between the cooking of the north and the south of France. Northern dishes rely more on the butter and cream produced in regions such as Normandy. However, each area has its own specialties. Close to the German

border, the northeastern regions of Alsace and Lorraine offer dishes such as sauerkraut, pork sausages, and pâtés. Mustard (from Dijon), beef, and wine grapes are abundant in Burgundy and are used in many dishes. One of the most famous is *boeuf à la borguignonne*, a beef stew cooked for hours in red wine.

In the south, dishes have Mediterranean influences and use olive oil, garlic, tomatoes, and seafood. In the southwest, force-fed geese produce foie gras, a delicious rich paste made from the liver. Another specialty is the black truffle, a very rare type

At left is an art nouveau–style dinner menu from the Splendid Hotel in Chatel-Guyon from 1904. France is considered by many gourmets to be the food center of the world. Pictured above is the famous bread known as *pain Poilâne*, sold in only one bakery in Paris.

A specially trained pig searches for truffles, a type of fungus that grows below the soil. Because truffles are difficult to harvest, they are considered a delicacy and are often very expensive.

of dark fungus. Meanwhile, white beans combined with pork and lamb are used to make cassoulet, a stew popular in the Languedoc region.

Eating Habits—A Typical French Meal

Few people take cooking—or eating—more seriously than the French. Eating well is extremely important to most French people, and they spend an amazing amount of time thinking about, talking about, and eating food.

Many techniques are used to prepare even the simplest French dishes. Some are complicated, while others take a great deal of time. In general, North Americans like meals that can be cooked as quickly and easily as possible. Many French, however, don't mind the effort or time that is involved in making the perfect meal. Cooking itself is an art form, and men, women, and even children learn how to prepare certain basic dishes such as crêpes and omelets.

Table Manners

Typically, a French lunch or dinner will begin with a starter or hors d'oeuvre, followed by a soup, a main course or entrée, a salad, a selection of cheeses, and, finally, dessert. Meals are always served with airy

A waiter prepares a dish at a customer's table at Le Train Bleu restaurant. The restaurant gets its name from the Blue Train, which once linked Paris to the French Riviera.

Ratatouille Provençale

In French, *ratouiller* means to shake and *tatouiller* means to stir. Put the two words together and you get ratatouille, a delicious stew from the sun-bathed Mediterranean region of France. Easy to make, this simple mixture is ideal in the summer.

Preparation

Heat a few tablespoons of good olive oil in a large pot. Add 2 chopped onions, 1 chopped green pepper, and 4 finely chopped garlic cloves. Stir for 2 minutes and then add 2 chopped eggplants, 4 chopped zucchini, and 3 to 4 chopped tomatoes. Add a pinch of thyme, a few sprigs of chopped parsley, a bay leaf, and salt and pepper to taste. Cook gently on low heat for 45 minutes. Ratatouille goes well with rice or an omelet. You can even spread it on toast.

white bread with a crunchy outer crust. This long stick of bread, known as a baguette (stick), can be bought fresh at numerous bakeries, or *boulangeries*. Instead of milk or soft drinks, French drink mineral water (flat or fizzy) and wine with their meals. All of this might seem like a lot of food, but portions in France are much smaller than in North America. This explains the mystery of why the French—despite eating such rich food—are much slimmer than North Americans. Also, the French hardly ever snack between meals and they rarely eat junk food.

When they do sit down to a meal, the French often remain at the table for hours. Lunches and dinners are not only for eating, but for drinking and talking as well. The French are great talkers. They love to passionately discuss everything from philosophy and politics to vacations.

Since the days of pre-Roman Gaul, the French have been extremely courageous eaters, attacking delicacies that would make North Americans squeamish. Popular foods include kidneys, brain, sweetbreads (pancreas), tripe, blood sausages, sheep's foot, tongue, intestines, and beef's testicles. Snails (*escargots*)

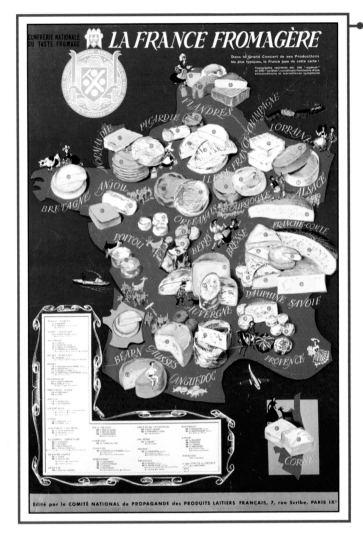

This poster advertises many types of French cheese. In France, there are cheeses that are used for sauces and cooking and others that are eaten plain or with bread. While the number of cheeses in France keeps growing, the old staples maintain their uniqueness.

are much loved, especially when cooked in butter and garlic. So are frogs' legs, which are similar in taste to tender chicken legs.

Cheeses

Officially, there are more than 400 types of French cheese, with new ones being invented every year. Some cheese recipes have been around for centuries, and they are guarded like precious secrets. Often, cheeses are named for the town or region from which they come. By law, they can only be made in that specific place. Producing a great cheese depends on many factors, ranging from the type of cows, goats, or sheep that supply the milk to the fields in which they graze.

Most restaurants and homes keep a well-stocked *plateau de fromages* (cheese board). These are kept at room temperature and served with bread. Neighborhood cheese shops, called *fromageries*, often sell more than 200 varieties. Most of the best-known cheeses are soft and runny. One of the most famous, Brie, comes from the northern Île-de-France and Champagne regions. Brie has been around since the fifteenth century. Normandy, with its many cows, is famous for cheeses such as Camembert. The Alpine regions produce harder cheeses

Cabernet Sauvignon vines are ready to be harvested in the St. Emilion region of Bordeaux, which is located in the west of France. Bordeaux produces the most wine in France and in the world. Bordeaux has about 7,000 châteaux or castles, each of which makes its own brand of wine. Cabernet Sauvignon is known as the king of red grapes.

such as Morbier, which is used in cheese fondue. Meanwhile, the Massif Central nurtures the cows that make Cantal and Roquefort, a tangy blue cheese. Also delicious is chèvre, a creamy cheese made from goat's milk.

Wines

The French believe that there is a suitable drink for every dish and every occasion. Before a meal, they often drink a light alcoholic beverage, called an aperitif. After meals, flavored liqueurs or cognacs known as *digestifs* are popular. During meals, the French drink wine—either white or red. In France, the least expensive wines, known as *vins de table* (table wines), are cheaper than Coca-Cola. However, even good wines are very affordable. And most French people know something about good wines and how to choose them.

Winemaking in France dates back to pre-Roman times. But it was the Romans who introduced the culture of making and drinking wine throughout ancient Gaul. Wine is made from the juice of freshly picked grapes, which have been left to settle in wooden barrels. Over time, the natural sugars in the grapes turn to alcohol.

France is covered with vineyards. Soil, temperature, sunlight, and many other factors contribute to the type and quality of a wine. So, of course, does the variety of grapes. The best wine-growing regions are Burgundy, Bordeaux, Provence, and Touraine. Burgundy and Bordeaux produce particularly famous strong red wines named after these regions. The vineyards of the northeastern Champagne region are responsible for the famous bubbly white wine known as Champagne.

DAILY LIFE AND CUSTOMS IN FRANCE

he French take enormous pride in their nationality. Most French people are extremely proud of the fact that their unique culture, history, and lifestyle have contributed so much to world civilization.

French Pride

In the eyes of people from other countries, however, this pride is sometimes seen as excessive. The French are sometimes called chauvinists, in the sense that they think everything French—from poetry and cinema to food and education—is the best in the world.

Anything that threatens centuries of tradition tends to put French people on the defensive. This is most apparent in France's relationship with the United States and American culture. On the one hand, the French are eternally grateful for America's aid, such as when U.S. troops helped liberate them from Nazi forces during World War II. And young people in particular love American movies, music, and television shows.

However, the invasion of American expressions (especially via the Internet) and American culture (including television shows such as *Friends*, fast food, Coca-Cola, and consumerism) concerns both the French government and many citizens. While most French appreciate American inventions

Pictured at left is a view of a charming cobblestone street in the Montmartre section of Paris, which is in the north of the city. The French are known for their love of pets, in particular, dogs and cats. It is not unusual to see small dogs and their owners sitting at cafés. Above, on the quays of the Seine, small bookstalls, called *bouquinistes*, sell books, old newspapers, and lithographs.

Many French people gather outside of a McDonald's restaurant in Marseille to participate in demonstrations against the American fast-food chain.

and ideas (particularly in areas of business and technology), some people have anti-American feelings.

French Manners and Mentality

In terms of behavior and attitudes, French people display an interesting mixture of formality and open-mindedness. Upon greeting each other, the French are very polite. They always address each other—in the street or on the phone, for example—using titles: Monsieur (sir), Madame (Madam), and Mademoiselle (Miss). They also have two forms of "you"—vous and tu. "Vous" is a more formal and polite version of "you." It is used by strangers or as a sign of respect. Workers call their bosses "vous," and children usually speak to grown-ups using "vous." "Tu" is a more casual form of "you" and is used by close colleagues or friends.

When visiting each other—particularly for a meal—French guests never show up empty-handed. Instead, they arrive with a bouquet of flowers or a decent bottle of wine. Men always shake hands with each other, while women give each other *bisous* (kisses) on the cheek. Depending on the region, the number of cheek kisses can range from two to four.

In this photograph, taken on August 13, 1953, in Grasse, French designer Christian Dior demonstrates shorter skirts to the public. The design, which was known as the New Look, scandalized many people.

This photograph of French designer Coco Chanel was taken by Henri Cartier-Bresson in 1964. Chanel introduced the idea of women wearing pants. Her women's suit designs also greatly influenced modern women's clothing styles.

Style and Attitudes

In a country famous for its fashion designers, it is not surprising that the French tend to dress very well. Both men and women are quite fashion conscious, and women in particular are known for their elegance and style. Use of perfume and cologne by both sexes is extremely common.

If in some ways the French seem more formal than North Americans, but in other ways, they are more casual. Attitudes toward sex and nudity, for example, are very carefree. Nudity on television and in films is seen as natural, as are sex scenes. In the summertime, French beaches are full of women who sunbathe topless.

Similarly, the French tend to be provocative in the sense that they enjoy and feel it is their right to challenge authority. Since the French Revolution, France has had an enormous number of popular uprisings. To this day, general strikes and protests are extremely frequent. Dissatisfied citizens from all walks of life take to the streets to show disagreement with decisions made by large businesses or the government.

Society of Opposites

French society in the twenty-first century is an interesting mixture of old and new tendencies. There is great respect for age-old ways of doing things—whether it is wearing a beret, handpicking grapes (instead of using a machine), or walking to the boulangerie to buy freshly baked bread. The French celebrate what they call their joie de vivre (joy of life). This means that more important than a successful career or making lots of money are simpler, more enjoyable things such as a two-hour four-course lunch or an afternoon spent arguing about politics in a sidewalk café.

While French cities continue to develop and modernize, their ancient squares and architecture are carefully preserved. Similarly, much is done (by both residents

A group of men come out to watch a game of *pétanque* in Aigues-Mortes, a village in Languedoc. Pétanque is played using metal balls that are rolled as closely as possible to a stationary wooden ball.

and governments) to protect the rural lifestyle of tiny villages and farms. This respect for the past goes hand in hand with a love of sophistication and novelty. Paris, for instance, is a cosmopolitan world capital that is always bubbling with new ideas and trends.

Pastimes

The importance of joie de vivre in French society means that the French take their leisure time very seriously. As in many European countries, soccer (which in France is called football or simply "foot") is probably the number one sport. Also popular are tennis (a French invention) and rugby. Bicycling is a much-loved pastime, and the famous monthlong Tour de France race in which cyclists race across France is a legendary event. A traditional game that is played in French villages and city squares by elderly men is *pétanque*.

The Alps and the Pyrenees provide fans of winter sports with many options, including some of the world's best skiing. Similarly, in summertime, the Atlantic and Mediterranean coasts offer everything from surfing to sailing.

Bikers race through the Alps during the annual Tour de France bicycle race. The race has been held every year since 1903, except for temporary suspensions during World Wars I and II. People from all over the world are allowed to participate in the race.

This still is from the 1967 film *Belle du Jour*. This famous movie was directed by Luis Buñuel, the founder of cinematic surrealism. The movie stars Catherine Deneuve, who is one of France's great actresses.

Culture

Culture is an essential priority for both the government and French citizens. Unlike the United States, where cultural institutions such as museums and theaters are private money-making businesses, in France, the government invests heavily in culture. For instance, many museums, such as the famous Louvre in Paris, are national museums that are operated by the government.

In general, the French tend to be passionate museum-goers. Paris alone has more than 100, ranging from the famous Louvre and the more contemporary art musuem, the Georges Pompidou Center, to small and unusual museums such as the Musée des Égouts (Museum of Sewers) and the Musée de la Serrure (Museum of Locks). France also boasts some of the best and most varied theater, dance, opera, and classical music in the world.

Then there is cinema, another French invention. After the United States and India, France has the largest and most important film industry in the world. For this reason, Paris is filled with more movie theaters than any other city on the planet. Everything from silent movies to contemporary foreign films to Hollywood blockbusters can be seen every day.

Former French actress and 1960s sex symbol Brigitte Bardot wades in the sea at Saint-Tropez while filming *Et Dieu . . . créa la Femme* (And God . . . Created Woman) in 1956.

EDUCATION AND WORK IN FRANCE

11

 raditionally, French schools were run by the Catholic religious orders such as the Dominicans and, later, the Jesuits.

Public Schools and Private Schools

Priests from the Dominican and Jesuit orders opened colleges and universities throughout France. Lessons were taught in Latin and French, and great emphasis was placed on religious subjects and a Christian view of the world.

After the French Revolution, the first public schools appeared. By 1905, when the separation of church and state became law, the French government created a system of free public education that was available to all French children.

At present, roughly 80 percent of French children go to public schools, while the remainder attend private (mostly Catholic) schools. In France, the public school system is paid for entirely by the government. All teachers, administrators, and school officials work for the Ministry of Education, making it the largest employer in France and the second largest government employer in the world (after the Russian army).

The Ministry of Education is responsible for making all decisions concerning education. These range from laws about attendance to hiring and training teachers

A poster advertises winter holidays in Cannes, a city on the French Riviera. Pictured above, French schoolchildren make the most of their recess by participating in group games. During the elementary school years (*école primaire*), French children are taught basic reading, writing, and arithmetic to prepare them for *lycèe*. School attendance is compulsory in France until the age of sixteen.

French high schoolers study philosophy in preparation for the Baccalauréat, a national test that will determine their academic futures.

and planning school curricula. For example, all students must study philosophy in their last year of high school (lycée). The French public school system is organized in a way that ensures that all students, no matter where they live, receive the same education and study the same subjects.

More than half of French children begin school by the age of two. At the age of three, almost all French kids are in school. They spend three years in *maternelle* (kindergarten) before moving on to primary school. Even during primary school, days are long. Classes run from 8 AM to 4 PM.

In France, where extracurricular activities are rare, school is all about schoolwork. Students work hard and high marks are difficult to come by. Grades are given on a scale from 0 to 20. However, getting a 20 or even an 18 or 19 is practically unheard of. Scoring 13 or 14 on a test is something to brag about.

From ages eleven to fifteen, children attend *collège*. During these years, students must decide what type of career they want to pursue. Teens who want to go to the university will go to a general lycée, where they study academic subjects such as literature and social sciences, while those interested in sciences will go to a technical lycée. Vocational lycées are for students who want to go to work after high school—in a business, for example. Currently, around 70 percent of French young people finish high school.

Students go to lycée between the ages of fifteen and eighteen. During the last year of lycée—known as *terminale*—the pressure is on, as students all over France prepare for a massive nationwide exam known as the Baccalauréat, or Bac. Since 1808, passing the Bac has been the only way to get into a university. Despite special schools that tutor students for the exam, every year around 40 percent of students who take it fail. Those who fail must wait until the following year to try again.

Universities and the Grandes Écoles

Those who pass the Bac can enroll in a university. Currently, about half of young French people attend a university. Since universities are public, they cost next to nothing. In fact, in 1995, French university students around the nation went on strike for a month to protest raising tuition fees that jumped from around US$50 to US$100 for a year.

Although they don't have the gyms, 24-hour libraries and computer rooms, and the diverse campus life that many North American universities boast, French universities have some of the world's leading professors and researchers on staff. French universities have a tradition of bringing together intellectuals from all over the world and creating an atmosphere of debate and exchange of ideas that is typically French. Paris's Sorbonne University, founded in 1257, is one of the world's most famous—not to mention oldest—universities.

While most students attend regular universities, a select few (less than 5 percent) go to the Grandes Écoles (Great Schools). The Grandes Écoles are small schools with a lot of money (some of which cost a lot of money) that

A large class meets in an auditorium for a lecture at Sorbonne University. The Sorbonne was founded by Robert de Sorbonne, a chaplain to King Louis IX of France.

are run separately from the rest of French public schools. There is fierce competition to get into them, as well as between the ambitious students who do attend them. But graduates of the Grandes Écoles are guaranteed success. Almost all of the leaders of government and major business corporations are graduates of the Grandes Écoles.

Three Grandes Écoles in particular stand above the rest. The École Polytechnique (called X) trains military and civil engineers. The École Normale Supérieure (Normal Sup) educates the country's most distinguished university professors. Meanwhile, many big executives and top-ranking government officials—including presidents, prime ministers, and most government ministers—are graduates of the École Nationale d'Administration (ENA).

Work and Unemployment

In general, French workers make less money than North Americans. However, they also work less. While the average American works between 1,900 and 2,000 hours a year, the average French person works between 1,600 and 1,700 hours. By law, all French workers enjoy five weeks of paid vacation a year (not including holidays). And since 1997, the workweek has been reduced from 40 hours a week to 35.

One of the reasons for this reduction was France's high rate of unemployment. Although it has fallen in the last few years, joblessness remains high, with 10 percent of workers unemployed. Fortunately, France is a country with generous social programs. Unemployed workers receive welfare benefits such as unemployment insurance as well as government-paid allowances for housing costs and family members.

Aside from free public education, French workers also enjoy good free or low-cost medical care (considered the best in the world by the World Health Organization), retirement plans, and inexpensive public housing. In fact, one in five French families lives in low-rent public housing, which is built and paid for by the government.

In the countryside, French farmers, fishermen, and other workers who make their living off the land also benefit from government aid and protections that allow them to work using the same traditional methods as their ancestors. Of course, this government aid is not free. The French pay some of the highest taxes in the world. However, most people agree that the protective social programs and quality of life offered by the government are worth it.

With the French state involved in so many aspects of French life, it is no wonder that more than 30 percent of the labor force (proudly) works for the government. In

Jasmine, a shrublike plant, is harvested at a small farm in the Alpes-Maritimes. There are more than 300 species of jasmine, which is often used for tea or perfume.

France, everything from education and transportation to postal and telecommunication services are run (usually quite efficiently) by the government.

The French Economy

After World War II, much of France was destroyed. For a while, living standards were quite low. However, in the late 1950s, 1960s, and 1970s, France grew and prospered as never before, becoming one of the richest and most important economies in Europe and the world. It developed its industries and went from being a backward, largely agricultural nation to a modern consumer society capable of producing its own goods and services. France currently boasts the fourth largest economy in the world after the United States, Japan, and Germany.

Today, France is a leader in industries ranging from transportation and telecommunications to chemical and pharmaceutical. It is one of the world centers for banking and insurance services. It is also the world's number one tourist destination. Every year, approximately 80 million foreign visitors come to France, particularly to visit Paris.

French industry is very diverse and employs all the latest technologies. That France is a leader in the technology field is hardly surprising. The nation spends more on research and development of new products and ideas than any country except for the United States and Japan. Since the 1960s, the government has been responsible for a number of very successful high-tech projects that have put France on the cutting edge of innovation. Before retiring in 2003, the Concorde was the world's fastest commercial jet, linking Paris and New York in three hours, and until recently, the TGV (Train à Grande Vitesse) was the world's fastest passenger train. The Chunnel (the tunnel running beneath the English Channel that links France and Britain), the Ariane space program, and the Minitel (the world's first public Internet-style system) were other French inventions that linked France to the rest of the world.

The sleek TGV train zips through the scenic French countryside. The TGV has recorded speeds of 320 mph (515 km/h), which set a worldwide record in 1990.

The French are also renowned for the traditional techniques and artistry with which they make some of the world's most sought-after luxury goods. French wines and spirits, such as cognac and Grand Marnier, are famous all over the globe. So are French perfumes, jewelry, fashions for men and women, fine leather goods, and glass, crystal, and porcelain objects. Many of these goods are still created by hand, using techniques that have been passed down through the centuries.

Similarly, many French farms and vineyards are small, family-run businesses that use traditional methods to produce high-quality goods such as cheeses and wines. Loved in France and exported throughout the world, these products make France the second largest exporter of agricultural products in the world.

The European Union

France emerged from World War II determined never to fight with its neighbors. All French governments have firmly believed that a unified federation of European nations would bring peace and security to Europe. Later, it was thought that such a union would also strengthen Europe economically, particularly with the growing power of the United States.

In 1957, France was one of six nations that made up the European Economic Community (EEC), a group of trading partners that developed common policies for trade, agriculture, and the transportation of goods. However, the plan was for European nations to join forces politically, socially, and economically.

Throughout the 1960s, 1970s, and 1980s, France was at the forefront of nations trying to build the European Union (EU). During these years, other countries joined the union (there are currently twenty-five member nations). In the

Joy, a perfume by Jean Patou, is the most expensive perfume in the world. The perfume is bottled by hand, which is done to prevent oxidation.

meantime, the European Union received its own governing bodies, the European Commission and Parliament, as well as its own Supreme Court of Justice and Central Bank. Borders between member nations were opened, and passports were no longer required to travel from one country to another. Citizens could move freely between nations, living and working wherever they pleased.

In 1999, a common currency called the Euro replaced the French franc as the national money. The franc had been in existence since its introduction in 1360 by King Jean le Bon (John the Good). The king needed some ransom money to be paid to the British who were holding him hostage (at the time, "franc" meant "free").

The Euro is the common currency used in the EU nations. And France is increasingly integrated with the rest of the Europe. For example, at present, 64 percent of its trade is carried out with other EU nations. Meanwhile, there are plans for a European Constitution that would set out common laws and rules for all member states.

As France moves into the twenty-first century, it confronts many of the same challenges it has faced throughout its history. How can it preserve its traditional past and culture while moving forward and embracing the changes of a rapidly changing world? How can it remain French and at the same time be part of a new, dynamic, and closely knit European community without borders? Although the future is unclear, it is certain that France will meet these challenges with all the flair, intelligence, and innovation that it has shown in the past. For its own good—and for the good of the rest of the world—it is certain that France will continue to play a leading role on the world stage in the years to come.

FRANCE
AT A GLANCE

HISTORY

The ancestors of today's French—the Celtic Gauls—arrived in France between 2000 and 1500 BC. After many conflicts, the Gauls were defeated by the Romans. By the fifth century, the Roman Empire had crumbled. The Franks and other Germanic peoples invaded the country. By then, Christianity was spreading through Europe. In 498, France's first king, Clovis, was baptized.

During the Middle Ages, France was governed by kings from the Merovingian, Carolingian, and Capetian dynasties. Under the Capetians, France prospered, although wars ravaged the country. French soldiers fought in the Crusades—holy wars that the Catholic Church waged against non-Christians. They also fought the English during the Hundred Years' War (1337–1453). The Wars of Religion (1562–1598) further threatened stability in the sixteenth century as Catholics persecuted Protestants. Later, King Henri IV granted religious, civil, and political rights to all French citizens.

In the seventeenth century, Kings Louis XIII and Louis XIV turned France into an absolute monarchy that was the most powerful kingdom in Europe. Louis XIV held court at the palace of Versailles. However, at the beginning of the eighteenth century, this old order was increasingly criticized. By the 1780s, most French citizens were fed up with Louis XVI. On July 14, 1789, the French Revolution began, and armed Parisians took to the streets and stormed the Bastille prison. In 1792, the First Republic was declared. During the next two years, thousands were unfairly arrested and led to the guillotine.

Order was restored when Napoléon Bonaparte came to power in 1799. Soon after crowning himself emperor, he decided to restore France to its former glory by invading all of Europe. His outsized ambitions led to enormous losses in battle and, finally, to his exile. However, he made many great contributions to France. One of the most important is the Napoleonic Code, the basis for the French legal system.

During the nineteenth century, France became industrialized, extended its colonies overseas, and created a separation between church and state. In the early twentieth century, World War I hit France very hard. The nation had barely recovered when World War II broke out. While Nazi troops occupied Paris and northern France, the pro-Nazi government ruled the rest of France. Meanwhile, in London, General Charles de Gaulle led the French Resistance movement. With the help of British and American forces, de Gaulle liberated France in 1944 and was elected president of the Fourth Republic.

During the 1950s and 1960s, France modernized and achieved great prosperity. At the same time, it gave up the last of its colonies—French Indochina and Algeria—in complicated wars. In May 1968, student protesters and striking workers demanding reforms shut down the country.

From 1981 to 1995, François Mitterand was France's president. A member of the Socialist Party, he opened the country to immigrants and promoted tolerance. In 1995, former Paris mayor Jacques Chirac became president. Under Chirac, France became fully integrated with the European Union, opening its frontiers and adopting the Euro as common currency.

ECONOMY

France has the fourth largest economy in the world in terms of GDP (gross domestic product, which is the total value of goods and services produced by a country in a year). It is a leader in many fields and industries, including transportation, telecommunications, banking, insurance, chemical, and pharmaceutical. It is the world's largest manufacturer of glass and a leader in the processing of aluminum, plastics, steel, and rubber. France is the world's fourth largest exporter of goods and the second largest supplier of service and agricultural products (cereals and foodstuffs such as sugar beets, oil seeds [sunflower seeds], dairy products, meat, wines, and alcoholic beverages). In terms of tourism, it is the most visited country in the world.

French industries are extremely sophisticated and technologically advanced. This is because the French spend more on research and development of new products and ideas than any country after Japan and the United States. At the same time, many of France's most famous products are based on traditional techniques and crafts. For centuries, French wines and other alcoholic beverages have been globally renowned, as have French-made luxury leather goods and fine glass and crystal. French perfumes, jewelry, and fashion—both ready-to-wear and haute couture—are famous throughout the world. Designers such as Chanel, Christian Dior, and Yves Saint Laurent are names associated with a style and glamour that are typically French.

Similarly, while France has a cutting-edge space program (Arianespace), it also proudly clings to centuries-old traditions. Most farms and vineyards are small, family-run enterprises that produce high-quality goods using traditional methods. Although this isn't the most inexpensive or most efficient means of production, the French government protects such farmers because these traditions are an important part of French culture and lifestyle.

Despite foreign pressure—mostly from the European Union—France refuses to abandon its traditional ways of doing things. Even so, as a leading trade partner of the European Union, France has opened up its frontiers to other EU products and investments. Currently 64 percent of France's imports and exports is traded with other EU nations, particularly Germany, Italy, the United Kingdom, Belgium, and Luxembourg. Its major non-EU trading partner is the United States.

Investors are drawn to France because of its healthy economy, stable currency, highly qualified workforce, and extremely modern infrastructure. The country boasts one of the world's most widespread and efficient transportation and telecommunications systems. Its system of roads and highways is the densest in the world and the longest in Europe. Its telephone networks are 95 percent digital. Energy production and distribution—half of which is produced domestically (76 percent is nuclear-generated)—is extremely efficient. Plus, workers enjoy great benefits, among them excellent health and welfare programs.

GOVERNMENT AND POLITICS

With the exception of a few brief periods, France has been a republic since the French Revolution of 1789 ended the system of monarchy. The First Republic was declared in 1792. Since then, France has had five different republics, each with its own constitution. The current Fifth Republic has been in existence since 1958.

France has a president, who is the head of state (or nation), and a prime minister, who is the head of the government. The current president is a former mayor of Paris, Jacques Chirac. The prime minister is Jean-Pierre Raffarin. Both took office in May 2002.

The president is elected directly by all French voters over the age of eighteen. Chirac is the first president to serve five years; before September 2000, the term was seven years. The president appoints the prime minister and, with the prime minister's recommendations, appoints the other members of the government. Among his duties, the president is in charge of the Council of Ministers and is the commander in chief of the armed forces. He is also responsible for representing France internationally: for signing agreements and treaties with foreign countries and greeting foreign leaders who visit France.

The prime minister is responsible for choosing members of government—ministers and secretaries of different sectors such as finance, culture, or transportation. Under the leadership of the prime minister, the government creates national policies and programs and is responsible for carrying them out. Both the prime minister and the government leaders he appoints are responsible for their actions to the Parliament.

The Parliament is made up of two assemblies. The National Assembly currently consists of 577 deputies. Deputies are elected directly by French citizens, and they represent the residents of their locality. The Senate is made up of 321 senators. Senators are elected, indirectly, for a period of nine years, with one-third up for reelection every three years. Aside from making sure the government administers the country well, the Parliament is responsible for drawing up and then voting upon legislation.

The French justice system is based on the Napoleonic Code established in the early nineteenth century. There are two kinds of courts in France. Civil courts rule on disputes between private individuals. Administrative courts rule on matters in which a public entity—a government agency, for example—is involved. The Napoleonic Code is the opposite of English-based American law: Under French law, a person charged with a crime is considered guilty until proven innocent. The highest court in the land—the equivalent of the Supreme Court—is the Conseil d'Etat. It has the final word on whether a government act is legal.

France has several major political parties that are represented in the government. On the right is the RPR (Rassemblement pour la République group). The largest centrist party is the UDF (Union pour la Démocratic Française). Meanwhile, to the left are the Socialists who believe in more liberal ideas. Further to the left is the Communist Party, while to the far right is the Front National, currently headed by Jean-Marie Le Pen, a controversial figure with a strong anti-immigrant stance.

TIMELINE

50,000 BC
Cro-Magnon Stone Age people leave cave paintings in southwest France.

52 BC
Roman conquest of Celtic Gaul.

754
Beginning of the Carolinginian dynasty.

843
Hugues Capet is the first king of the Capetian dynasty. The Catholic Church becomes very wealthy and influential. The Crusades are fought against non-Christians.

1500 BC
Celts begin to arrive in France (Gaul) from northern and central Europe.

AD 507
Franks from Germany invade Gaul, which becomes France. The first French king, Clovis, makes Paris his capital. Beginning of the Merovingian dynasty.

1598
Edict of Nantes grants religious freedom to all.

1643
King Louis XIV comes to power. France becomes the most powerful nation in Europe, and French culture spreads throughout the continent.

1792
Declaration of the First Republic. Beginning of the Reign of Terror under the leadership of the radical Jacobins.

1610
King Louis XIII comes to power. With the aid of Cardinal Richelieu, France becomes an absolute monarchy.

1789
Armed citizens take to the streets of Paris and storm the Bastille prison. Beginning of the French Revolution.

1799
Napoléon Bonaparte comes to power. In 1804, he crowns himself emperor of France.

1918
With the end of World War I, Alsace and Lorraine are returned to France.

1945
Supported by British and American troops, de Gaulle's French troops liberate Paris.

1946
The Fourth Republic is declared with de Gaulle as president. Reconstruction begins.

1914
Outbreak of World War I. France is devastated, and more than 1 million men are killed.

1939
Outbreak of World War II. Hitler's Nazi forces occupy France. General de Gaulle leads the Resistance from London.

1958
The Fifth Republic is declared, and de Gaulle returns to power.

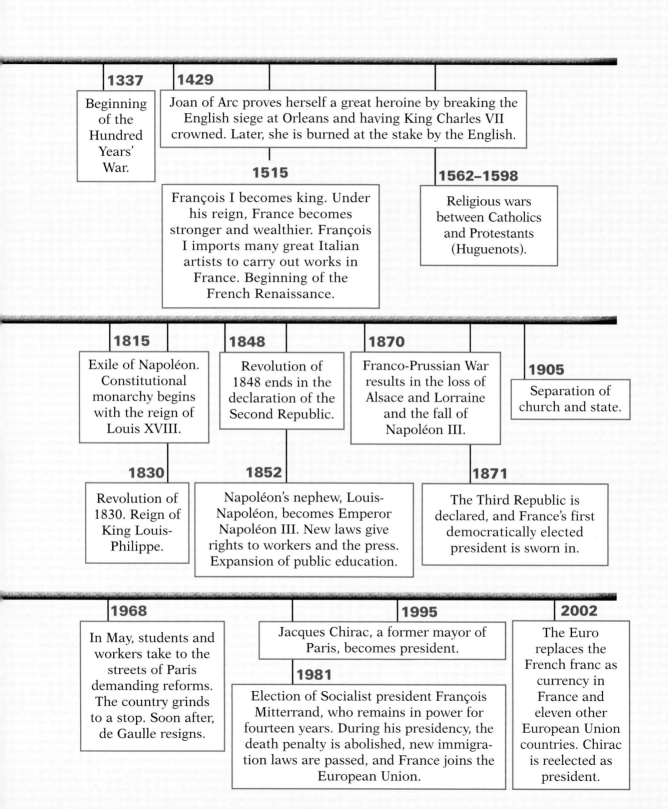

1337
Beginning of the Hundred Years' War.

1429
Joan of Arc proves herself a great heroine by breaking the English siege at Orleans and having King Charles VII crowned. Later, she is burned at the stake by the English.

1515
François I becomes king. Under his reign, France becomes stronger and wealthier. François I imports many great Italian artists to carry out works in France. Beginning of the French Renaissance.

1562–1598
Religious wars between Catholics and Protestants (Huguenots).

1815
Exile of Napoléon. Constitutional monarchy begins with the reign of Louis XVIII.

1848
Revolution of 1848 ends in the declaration of the Second Republic.

1870
Franco-Prussian War results in the loss of Alsace and Lorraine and the fall of Napoléon III.

1905
Separation of church and state.

1830
Revolution of 1830. Reign of King Louis-Philippe.

1852
Napoléon's nephew, Louis-Napoléon, becomes Emperor Napoléon III. New laws give rights to workers and the press. Expansion of public education.

1871
The Third Republic is declared, and France's first democratically elected president is sworn in.

1968
In May, students and workers take to the streets of Paris demanding reforms. The country grinds to a stop. Soon after, de Gaulle resigns.

1995
Jacques Chirac, a former mayor of Paris, becomes president.

2002
The Euro replaces the French franc as currency in France and eleven other European Union countries. Chirac is reelected as president.

1981
Election of Socialist president François Mitterrand, who remains in power for fourteen years. During his presidency, the death penalty is abolished, new immigration laws are passed, and France joins the European Union.

FRANCE

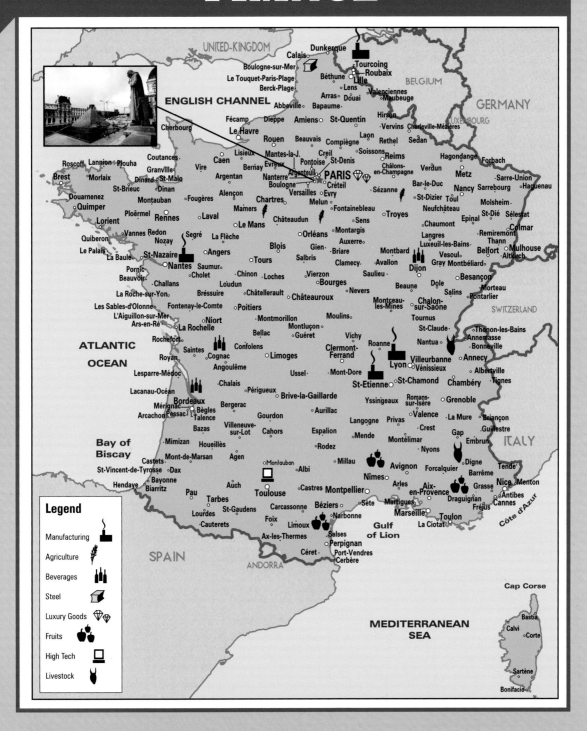

UNITED-KINGDOM
Calais
Dunkerque
Boulogne-sur-Mer
Tourcoing
Roubaix
BELGIUM
Le Touquet-Paris-Plage
Béthune
Lille
GERMANY
Berck-Plage
Lens
Valenciennes
LUXEMBOURG
Arras
Douai
Maubeuge
ENGLISH CHANNEL
Abbeville
Bapaume
Hirson
Fécamp
Dieppe
Amiens
St-Quentin
Charleville-Mézières
Cherbourg
Rouen
Beauvais
Compiègne
Laon
Vervins
Sedan
Roscoff
Lannion
Plouha
Coutances
Lisieux
Mantes-la-J.
Creil
Soissons
Reims
Hagondange
Forbach
Brest
Morlaix
Granville
Vire
Caen
Bernay
Evreux
Pontoise
St-Denis
Châlons-en-Champagne
Verdun
Metz
Sarre-Union
Dinard
St-Malo
Argentan
Nanterre
Argenteuil
PARIS
Bar-le-Duc
Nancy
Sarrebourg
Haguenau
St-Brieuc
Dinan
Boulogne
Créteil
Evry
St-Dizier
Toul
Douarnenez
Montauban
Alençon
Versailles
Sézanne
Neufchâteau
Molsheim
St-Dié
Sélestat
Quimper
Ploërmel
Fougères
Mamers
Chartres
Melun
Fontainebleau
Troyes
Chaumont
Epinal
Colmar
Lorient
Laval
Le Mans
Châteaudun
Sens
Langres
Remiremont
Thann
Mulhouse
Quiberon
Vannes
Redon
Segré
La Flèche
Orléans
Montargis
Auxerre
Luxeuil-les-Bains
Belfort
Altkirch
Le Palais
Nozay
Angers
Blois
Gien
Briare
Montbard
Vesoul
Gray
Montbéliard
La Baule
St-Nazaire
Tours
Salbris
Clamecy
Avallon
Dijon
Besançon
Pornic
Nantes
Saumur
Cholet
Chinon
Loches
Vierzon
Bourges
Beaune
Dole
Salins
Morteau
Beauvoir
Challans
Loudun
Châtellerault
Nevers
Saulieu
Pontarlier
La Roche-sur-Yon
Bréssuire
Châteauroux
Montceau-les-Mines
Chalon-sur-Saône
Les Sables-d'Olonne
Fontenay-le-Comte
Poitiers
Tournus
SWITZERLAND
L'Aiguillon-sur-Mer
Niort
Montmorillon
Moulins
St-Claude
Thonon-les-Bains
Ars-en-Ré
Bellac
Montluçon
Guéret
Vichy
Nantua
Annemasse
Bonneville
ATLANTIC
Rochefort
Confolens
Clermont-Ferrand
Roanne
Lyon
Villeurbanne
Annecy
OCEAN
Royan
Saintes
Cognac
Limoges
Vénissieux
Albertville
Angoulême
Ussel
Mont-Dore
St-Etienne
St-Chamond
Chambéry
Vignes
Lesparre-Médoc
Chalais
Périgueux
Brive-la-Gaillarde
Yssingeaux
Romans-sur-Isère
Grenoble
Lacanau-Océan
Bordeaux
Bergerac
Gourdon
Aurillac
Valence
La Mure
Briançon
Mérignac
Bègles
Talence
Villeneuve-sur-Lot
Cahors
Espalion
Langogne
Privas
Crest
Guillestre
Arcachon
Pessac
Bazas
Rodez
Mende
Montélimar
Gap
Embrun
Mimizan
Houeillès
Agen
Millau
Nyons
Digne
Tende
Bay of
Biscay
Castets
Mont-de-Marsan
Montauban
Albi
Nîmes
Avignon
Forcalquier
Barrème
St-Vincent-de-Tyrosse
Dax
Castres
Montpellier
Arles
Aix-en-Provence
Grasse
Nice
Menton
Hendaye
Bayonne
Auch
Toulouse
Sète
Martigues
Draguignan
Antibes
Cannes
Biarritz
Pau
Tarbes
Béziers
Marseille
Fréjus
Côte d'Azur
Lourdes
St-Gaudens
Carcassonne
Narbonne
Toulon
La Ciotat
Foix
Limoux
Gulf
of Lion
Cauterets
Ax-les-Thermes
Salses
Perpignan
SPAIN
Céret
Port-Vendres
Cerbère
ANDORRA

Legend

- ⚒ Manufacturing
- 🌾 Agriculture
- 🍾 Beverages
- ◨ Steel
- 💎 Luxury Goods
- 🍎 Fruits
- 💻 High Tech
- 🐄 Livestock

MEDITERRANEAN
SEA

Cap Corse

Bastia
Calvi
Corte
Sartène
Bonifacio

ECONOMIC FACT SHEET

GDP: 1,460 billion Euros

GDP Sectors: Agriculture 3%, industry 26%, services 71%

Land Use: Farm land 60%, woods and forests 29%

Currency: Euro; 1 Euro = US$1.15

Workforce: Services 71%, industry 26%, agriculture 3%

Major Agricultural Products: Sugar beets, beef and veal, cereals, oil seeds, confectionery (candy and pastry), soft drinks, wine, and alcoholic beverages. (France is the second largest producer of food products in the EU.)

Major Exports: U.S. $307.8 billion; machinery and transportation equipment, aircraft, plastics, chemicals, pharmaceutical products, iron and steel, beverages

Major Imports: U.S. $303.7 billion; machinery and equipment, vehicles, crude oil, aircraft, plastics, chemicals

Significant Trading Partners:

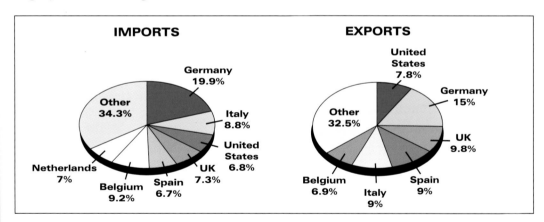

Rate of Unemployment: Approximately 9%

Roads and Highways: The largest system in the EU.

Railroads: Total of 20,308 miles (32,682 km) of railroad tracks

Waterways and Ports: Total of 9,278 miles (14,932 km). Marseilles is the largest port in France and on the Mediterranean Sea and the third largest in Europe.

Airports: Total 477 (paved 273, unpaved 204)

POLITICAL FACT SHEET

Official Country Name: République Française (French Republic)

Capital: Paris

System of Government: Republic

Executive Structure: Executive power is shared between the president (the head of France) and the prime minister (the head of the French government).

Legislative Structure: Legislative power is carried out in a Parliament, made up of the National Assembly (currently with 577 elected deputies) and the Senate (currently with 321 elected senators).

Motto: Liberté, Egalité, Fraternité (Liberty, Equality, Brotherhood)

Administrative Divisions: The French Republic is made up of metropolitan France, which is divided into twenty-two regions and subdivided into ninety-six departments, along with four overseas departments (DOM; Guadeloupe, Martinique, French Guiana, and Réunion), four overseas territories (TOM; French Polynesia, New Caledonia and Wallis, and Futuna), the French Southern and Antarctic Territories, and two "territorial collectivities" with a special status (Mayotte and St. Pierre and Miquelon).

Constitution: The Constitution of October 4, 1958, provides the foundation for France's Fifth Republic.

Legal System: Civil law system based on Napoleonic Code

Voting Age: Eighteen

National Anthem: "La Marseillaise," by Captain Rouget de Lisle, written in 1792 (in twenty hours) during the middle of the French Revolution.

Into the fight we too shall enter,
When our fathers are dead and gone;
We shall find their bones laid down to rest,
With the fame of their glories won,
Oh, to survive them care we not,
Glad are we to share their grave,
Great honor is to be our lot
To follow or to venge our brave.

CULTURAL FACT SHEET

Official Language: French

Major Religions: Roman Catholic 81.4%, Muslim 6.89%, Protestant 1.64%, Jewish 1.29%, other 8.12%

Population: 60,180,529

Ethnic Groups: Celtic and Latin, with Teutonic, Slavic, North African, Indochinese, and Basque minorities

Life Expectancy: Men 75 years, women 83 years

Time: Greenwich Mean Time plus 1 hour

Literacy Rate: 99%

National Flower: Fleur-de-lys (lily)

National Bird: Rooster

Cultural Leaders:

    Visual and Decorative Arts: Henri Matisse (artist), Jean Dubuffet (artist), Henri Cartier-Bresson (photographer), Yves Saint Laurent (fashion designer), Coco Chanel (fashion designer)

    Literature: Jean-Paul Sartre, Albert Camus, Marguerite Duras, Simone de Beauvoir, Françoise Sagan, Victor Hugo

    Entertainment (Film and Music): Jean-Luc Godard (film director), François Truffaut (film director), Catherine Deneuve (actress), Gerard Dépardieu (actor), Jacques Brel (composer/singer), Serge Gainsbourg (composer/singer), Edith Piaf (singer), Jeanne Moreau (actress/singer)

    Sports: Yannick Noah (tennis), Zinédine Zidane (soccer), Michel Platini (soccer), Alain Prost (Grand Prix race car driving), Bernard Hinault (cyclist)

National Holidays and Festivals

France has both national holidays and religious (Catholic) holidays. Some fall on specific dates each year. Others move around from year to year.

January 1: **New Year's Day**	July 14: **Bastille Day**
April: **Easter**	August 15: **Assumption of the Blessed**
April: **Easter Monday**	**Virgin Mary**
May 1: **Labor Day**	November 1: **All Saints' Day**
May 8: **World War II Victory Day**	November 11: **Armistice Day**
May: **Ascension (l'Ascencion)**	December 25: **Christmas Day**
May/June: **Pentecost**	

GLOSSARY

absolute monarchy (ab-suh-LOOT MAH-nar-kee) A government run by an all-powerful king or queen, believed to be linked to God.

anti-Semitic (an-ti-seh-MIH-tik) Having racist views or attitudes toward Jews.

backlash (BAK-lash) A strong reaction against a political or social act.

beret (buhr-AY) A woolen cap with a tight headband and a soft, full, flat top.

boar (BOR) A wild pig.

brothel (BRA-thul) A building in which prostitutes are available.

Celts (KEHLTS) An early group of people that migrated to France from northern and central Europe.

chauvinist (SHO-vih-nist) Someone with an extreme sentiment of patriotism or a feeling that his or her group or place is superior to others.

Communism (KAH-myoo-nis-um) A political system in which there is no private property and goods are commonly owned by everyone.

constitutional monarchy (kon-stih-TOO-shuh-nul MAH-nar-kee) A government run by a king or queen based on a written constitution.

consumerism (kun-SOO-mer-ih-zum) A preoccupation with and desire for buying consumer goods.

cosmopolitan (koz-muh-POH-li-tuhn) Having worldly sophistication.

Crusades (kroo-SAYDZ) Military expeditions undertaken by Christian powers in the Middle Ages to win the Holy Land from the Muslims.

cuisine (kwih-ZEEN) A style of cooking.

dialect (DY-uh-lekt) The ways in which a language is spoken in different regions.

druid (DROO-id) A Celtic religious priest or healer, often believed to have magical powers.

dynasty (DY-nuh-stee) An influential group, such as a royal family, that stays in power for a long time.

edict (EE-dihkt) A declaration that becomes law.

enlightened (en-LY-tend) Having great understanding and progressive views.

exile (EG-zyl) A period of forced absence from one's home or country.

farce (FARS) An absurdity or joke.

frigid (FRIH-jid) Extremely cold.

Gothic (GAH-thik) A style of architecture invented in twelfth-century northern France.

guillotine (GIH-lih-teen) A machine for executing people by cutting off their heads with a heavy metal blade.

haute couture (OHT coo-TYUR) Exclusive fashions for women created by Parisian fashion designers.

Huguenots (HYOO-geh-nahts) French Protestants (particularly of the sixteenth and seventeenth centuries).

King Arthur (KING AHR-thur) A legendary English king who inspired courtly tales of knights and ladies.

Left (LEHFT) A group with political views or ideas that support change of established policies and increased liberty and rights.

mosaic (moh-ZAY-ik) A picture made by fitting together small pieces of stone, glass, or ceramic tile.

mosque (MAHSK) A place of worship and prayer for Muslims.

ornamental (or-nuh-MEN-tal) Decorative.

ornate (OR-nayt) Elaborately decorated.

patent (PA-tint) A legal document that stops people from copying an invention.

radicals (RAH-dih-kulz) People who desire large political changes.

ransom (RAN-suhm) The price paid to rescue someone who is being held prisoner.

Reformation (reh-for-MAY-shun) The time during the sixteenth century when many people rejected the beliefs of the Catholic Church and turned to the teachings of the Protestant Church.

sauerkraut (SOW-er-krowt) A dish of shredded and salted cabbage flavored by its own juices.

sauté (sah-TAY) To fry in a little butter or oil.

secular (SE-kyuh-lur) Not religious.

Socialism (SOH-shuh-li-zim) A system in which the means of production are owned and controlled by the state (government).

sonnet (SAH-neht) A fourteen-line rhyming poem.

stake (STAYK) A wooden post to which a person is bound for execution by burning.

vocational (vo-KAY-shuh-nuhl) Relating to training in a skill or trade to be pursued as a career.

welfare (WEHL-fayr) Aid in the form of money or necessities for those in need.

FOR MORE INFORMATION

American Association of Teachers of
  French (AATF)
Southern Illinois University
Carbondale, IL 62901-4510
(618) 453-5731
Web site: http://frenchteachers.org

Cultural Service at the French Embassy
972 Fifth Avenue
New York, NY 10021
(212) 439-1400
Web site: http://www.frenchculture.org

Embassy of France
4101 Reservoir Road NW
Washington, DC 20007
(202) 944-6000
Web site: http://www.info-france-usa.org

Federation of Alliances Françaises
  (USA), Inc.
4101 Reservoir Road NW

Washington, DC 20007
(202) 944-6351
Web site: http://www.afusa.org

French Government Tourist Office
La Maison Française
4101 Reservoir Road
Washington, DC 20007
(202) 944-6090 or 944-6134
Web site: http://www.la-maison-
  francaise.org

Web Sites

Due to the changing nature of Internet
links, the Rosen Publishing Group, Inc.,
has developed an online list of Web
sites related to the subject of this book.
This site is updated regularly. Please use
this link to access the list:

http://www.rosenlinks.com/pswc/fran

FOR FURTHER READING

Bernstein, Richard. *Fragile Glory: A Portrait of France and the French.* New York: Knopf, 1990.

Blume, Mary. *A French Affair: The Paris Beat 1965–1998.* New York: The Free Press, 1999.

Corbett, James. *Through French Windows: An Introduction to France in the Nineties.* Ann Arbor, MI: University of Michigan Press, 1994.

Dickens, Charles. *Dickens in France: Selected Pieces by Charles Dickens on France and the French.* Brighton, U.K.: In Print Publishing Ltd., 1996.

Fisher, M. F. K. *Long Ago in France.* New York: Simon & Schuster, 1991.

Flanner, Janet. *Paris Was Yesterday, 1925–1939.* New York: Penguin, 1981.

Freson, Robert. *The Taste of France.* New York: Stewart, Tabori & Chang, 1998.

Kerper, Barrie. *Paris—The Collected Traveler: An Inspired Anthology & Travel Resource.* New York: Three Rivers Press, 2000.

Twain, Mark. *The Innocents Abroad.* New York: Collins, 1920.

BIBLIOGRAPHY

Académie Française. Retrieved July 2003 (http://www.academie-francaise.fr).

An American in Paris Web site. Retrieved June 2003 (http://perso.club-internet.fr/hwelty/index.html).

Astérix International. Retrieved July 2003 (http://www.astérix-international.de).

Baillie, Kate, and Tim Salmon. *The Rough Guide to France.* New York: Rough Guides, 2001.

CIA. The World Factbook, 2002—France. Retrieved July 2003 (http://www.cia.gov/cia/publications/factbook/geos/fr.html).

DiscoverFrance.net. Retrieved June 2003 (http://www.discoverfrance.net).

Dorling Kindersley Publishing Staff. *Eyewitness Travel Guide to France.* London: Dorling Kindersley Publishing, 1998.

Égide: Centre français pour l'accueil et les échanges internationaux (French center for international study and exchanges). Retrieved July 2003 (http://www.egide.asso.fr/uk/guide/connaitre/culture).

Embassy of France in the U.S. Retrieved June 2003 (http://www.info-france-usa.org).

Flags of the World: France. Retrieved July 2003 (http://www.crwflags.com/fotw/flags/fr-reg.html).

Focus Magazine Online. Retrieved June 2003 (http://www.focusmm.com/france/fr_anamn.htm).

France.com. Retrieved June 2003 (http://www.france.com).

Michelin Travel Publications Staff. *The Green Guide: France.* Watford, UK: Michelin Travel Publications, 2001.

Gurfinkiel, Michel. "Islam in France: The French Way of Life Is in Danger." *Middle East Quarterly*, Volume IV, Number 1, March 1997. Retrieved July 2003 (http://www.meforum.org/article/337).

Hyman, Paula E. *The Jews of Modern France.* Berkeley, CA: University of California Press, 1998.

La Légende de Tristan et Iseulte. Retrieved July 2003 (http://www.geocities.com/conseilculturel/Iseult.htm).

Michaud, Guy, and Alain Kimmel. *Le Nouveau Guide France.* Paris: Hachette, 1994.

Official French Tourist Office. Retrieved June 2003 (http://www.franceguide.com/home.asp?m1=9).

Oliver, Jeanne. *Lonely Planet Guide to France.* London: Lonely Planet, 2003.

Tlemçani, Rachid. "Islam in France: The French Have Themselves to Blame." *Middle East Quarterly*, Volume IV, Number 1, March 1997. Retrieved July 2003 (http://www.meforum.org/article/338).

PRIMARY SOURCE
IMAGE LIST

Cover, page 23 (bottom): Letter from Joan of Arc to Count of Dunois, March 20, 1466.

Page 15: Hand-colored 1724 map of France by Alexis Hubert Jaillot. Housed at the Library of Congress Geography and Map Division, Washington, D.C.

Page 18: *The Declaration of the Rights of Man and of the Citizen*, 1789 oil on canvas painting by the French School. Housed at the Musée de la Ville de Paris, Musée Carnavalet, Paris.

Page 19: French poster from 1792 illustrating "Liberté, Egalité, Fraternité" (Liberty, Equality, and Brotherhood).

Page 21: Detail of a late-fourteenth-century illuminated manuscript, *Les Grandes Chroniques de France*, of the Bishop of Rheims baptizing and anointing Clovis I, king of the Franks. Housed at the Bibliothèque Municipale in Castres, France.

Page 22 (top): Housed at the Musée du Louvre in Paris, a circa 1365 to 1367 fleur-de-lys clasp made of gold and precious jewels said to have belonged to King Louis IX. Photo by Peter Willi.

Page 22 (bottom): Fifteenth-century illuminated manuscript depicting a military procession leaving a fortress. From volume four of *The Chronicles* by Froissart. Housed at the British Library, London.

Page 23 (top): German tapestry illustrating the arrival of Joan of Arc at the Château de Chinon in 1428.

Page 24: Portrait of François I, king of France, by Jean Clouet. Housed at the Musée du Louvre, Paris.

Page 25: Portrait of Louis XIV, king of France, by Hyacinthe Rigaud. Housed at the Musée du Louvre, Paris.

Page 26: Hall of Mirrors (La Galerie des Glaces) at the Château of Versailles, designed by Louis LeVau.

Page 27 (top): Colored lithograph illustrating the storming of the Bastille, published by Imagerie Pellerin on July 14, 1880, in celebration of the anniversary of the French Revolution.

Page 27 (bottom): Engraving from the *Revolutionary Calendar for Year II of the Republic* (1794). Housed at Musée Carnavalet, Paris.

Page 28: French Constitution of 1791, signed by King Louis XVI in left-hand margin on September 3, 1791.

Page 29: Circa 1793 French print of the execution of Marie Antoinette on the Place de la Revolution.

Page 30 (top): *Napoléon Crossing Mount Saint Bernard*, 1810 French painting by Jacques-Louis David, housed at Malmaison Castle, France.

Page 30 (bottom): April 2, 1810, marriage certificate of Napoléon Bonaparte, emperor of France. Housed at the Napoleonic Museum, Rome.

Page 31: Portrait of architect Gustave Eiffel in front of incomplete Eiffel Tower, dated July 1888.

Page 32: July 15, 1940, photograph of Adolf Hitler, Professor Giesel, Professor Speer, and Professor Breker in front of the Eiffel Tower.

Page 33: Front cover of the *Paris Soir* newspaper dated August 4, 1940, declaring that General Charles de Gaulle is condemned to death. From Les Archives de Gaulle, Paris.

Page 34: May 13, 1959, Associated Press photo of Muslim women demonstrating against the Fourth French Republic's policies against the Algerian Nationalist Revolt.

Page 35 (top): Photo of students rioting in Paris on rue Guy Lussac on May 11, 1968.

Page 35 (bottom): Photo of battles between police and students in Paris on May 7, 1968.

Page 36: May 1, 2002, photo by Daniel Gillet of an anti–Jean-Marie Le Pen demonstration in Paris.

Page 37: April 2, 2002, portrait of Jacques Chirac, president of France, by Antonio Scattolon.

Page 38: Tablet inscribed with speech written by Roman emperor Claudius in AD 48. Housed in the Museo della Civilta Romana, in Rome.

Page 39: *Breviarie de Belleville*, a 1343 French illuminated manuscript page featuring miniatures by Jean Pucelle. Housed in the Bibliothèque Nationale, Paris.

Page 40: Circa 1636 portrait of Cardinal Richelieu by Philippe de Champaigne. Housed at the Musée Condé, Chantilly, France.

Page 43: A page from *Le Petit Nicholas*, published in 1960, by Jean-Jacques Sempé and René Goscinny.

Page 44: A page from the fourteenth-century manuscript *Le Roman de Lancelot du Lac*. Housed at the Pierpont Morgan Library, New York.

Page 46: Late-fifteenth-century illuminated manuscript page from *Le Roman de Tristan*. Housed at the Musée Condé, Chantilly, France.

Page 47: Early-fifteenth-century medieval casket lid featuring one of the earliest-known medieval representations of the *Romance of Tristan and Isolde*. Housed in the British Museum, London.

Page 48 (top): Engraving by Gaston Gelibert from "The Hare and the Tortoise," from Jean de La Fontaine's *Fables*.

Page 48 (bottom): Color engraving by Félix Lorioux for title page of Jean de La Fontaine's *Fables*. From a private collection.

Page 49 (top): Illustration of Obelix from René Gasconny and Albert Uderzo's comic book, *Astérix et la Rentrée Gauloise*.

Page 49 (bottom): Illustration of Astérix from René Gasconny and Albert Uderzo's comic book, *Astérix et la Rentrée Gauloise*.

Page 51: Photo by Topham of the liberation of Paris in 1944.

Page 52: Photo of Good Friday procession in Perpignon, France, on April 21, 2000.

Page 54 (top): August 29, 1944, photo of Parisians marching toward the Arc de Triomphe in celebration of the liberation of Paris.

Page 58 (top): A January 1922 illustration of French Druids from *Le Pelerin*, a Catholic weekly magazine. Housed at the Mary Evans Picture Library.

Page 58 (bottom): Fifteenth-century French illuminated manuscript depicting St. Louis leaving for the Crusades.

Page 61: Circa 1434 painting by Roger van der Weyden entitled *The Altar of the Last Judgement*. Housed in the Hôtel-Dieu in Beaune, France.

Page 62 (top): François Dubois's painting *Saint Bartholomew's Day Massacre*, August 24, 1572. Housed at the Musée des Beaux Arts, in Lausanne, France.

Page 62 (bottom): Sixteenth-century French School painting of Henri IV, king of Navarre. Housed at Château de Pau, France.

Page 63: Page from the 1598 Edict of Nantes, by the French School. Housed at the Centre Historique des Archives Nationales in Paris.

Page 64 (top): Letter dated January 24, 1895, from Captain Alfred Dreyfus to his wife from the prison at Saint Martin de Re.

Page 64 (bottom): *Le Traitre* (The Traitor), 1899 French caricature of Alfred Dreyfus, from a series of posters called "Musée des Horreurs."

Page 66: *Icarus*, from Henri Matisse's Jazz series, Paris, 1947. Housed in the Spencer Collection, the New York Public Library, New York.

Page 68 (top): Photo of rock painting of leaping cow and small horses, circa 13,000 BC in the Lascaux caves in Dordogne, France.

Page 68 (bottom): Photo of the second-century Roman amphitheater in Arles, France.

Page 69: Photo by Peter Willi of Notre-Dame de Paris, which was completed in 1345.

Page 70: Thirteenth-century stained-glass rose and lancet windows of north wall of Chartres Cathedral, Chartres, France.

Page 71: June 1965 photo by Charles Rotkin of Château de Chambord, in Blois, France.

Page 72: Eighteenth-century undated painting, *Shepherdess Seated with Sheep and a Basket of Flowers near a Ruin in a Wooded Landscape*, by Jean-Honoré Fragonard.

Page 73 (top): *Water Lilies*, oil on canvas painting dated 1914–1917, by Claude Monet. Housed in the Musée Marmottan, Paris.

Page 74 (top): Circa 1889 self-portrait of Vincent van Gogh. Oil on canvas. Housed at the Musée d'Orsay, Paris.

Page 74 (bottom): Portrait of Paul Gauguin in front of one of his Tahitian paintings. From a private collection.

Page 75: *Balzac*, sculpture by Auguste Rodin. From Musée Rodin, Paris.

Page 76 (top): July 14, 1989, photo of the Eiffel Tower by Mark Antman.

Page 76 (bottom): *Tahitian Idyll*, 1892 oil on canvas painting by Paul Gauguin. Housed in the Hermitage, St. Petersburg, Russia.

Page 77: *Les Demoiselles D'Avignon*, 1907 painting by Pablo Picasso. Housed at the Museum of Modern Art, New York.

Page 78 (top): Yves Klein painting, *International Klein Blue*, painted between 1956 and 1962.

Page 78 (bottom): Photo of Abbesses Métro station entrance in Montmartre, Paris, designed by Hector Guimard.

Page 79: Photo of La Chapelle de Notre-Dame de Haut in Ronchamp, France, designed by Le Corbusier, 1955.

Page 80: First-edition title page of Molière's *Les Précieuses Ridicules*.

Page 81: Fifteenth-century manuscript illustration "The Lover and the God of Love" from *Roman de la Rose* (Romance of the Rose) by Guillaume de Lorris.

Page 82: Late-nineteenth-century poster, designed by Paul Berthon, for a film based on Jean Racine's play *Athalie*. From Bibliothèque Nationale, Paris.

Page 83: June 21, 1964, photo of Douglas Rain performing in Molière's play *Le Bourgeois Gentilhomme* at the Stratford Festival in Ontario, Canada.

Page 84 (top): *Jean-Philippe Rameau with a Violin*, painting by Jacques Andre Joseph Camelot Aved. Housed in the Musée des Beaux-Arts, Dijon, France.
Page 85 (bottom): Circa 1870 photogravure by Goupil of French writer Victor Hugo.
Page 87: Circa 1835 to 1845 photograph of French author Honoré de Balzac, taken in Paris.
Page 88: Undated photo by Bruno Babey of Jean-Paul Sartre and Simone de Beauvoir, taken in Paris.
Page 89: Sheet music cover by R. de Valerio, 1923. Josephine Baker doing the Charleston at the Folies Bergères in Paris. Published by Editions Francis Salabert.
Page 90: Dinner menu from 1904 at the Splendid Hotel in Chetal-Guyon, France. Menu features filet of roast beef, braised chicory, and lemon ice cream.
Page 91: March 2002 photo by Annie Sommers of *pain Poilâne* at Boulangerie Poilâne, number 8 rue du Cherche-Midi, Paris.
Page 94: Twentieth-century color lithograph (poster)

La France Fromagère. Housed at the Bibliothèque-Musée Fornay, Paris.
Page 97: March 2002 photo by Annie Sommers of a *bouqiniste* (bookseller) by the Seine, in Paris.
Page 98: August 13, 1953, photograph of French designer Christian Dior and model in Grasse, France.
Page 99: Henri Cartier-Bresson photo of French designer Coco Chanel in Paris, 1964.
Page 101 (top): Photo of actress Catherine Deneuve in 1967 French film *Belle de Jour* (Beauty of the Day), directed by Luis Buñuel. Image Property of National Screen Service Corp.
Page 102: Circa 1892 colored lithograph (poster) by Emmanuel Brun advertising the Casino des Fleurs, in Cannes, in the winter. Housed at the Bibliothèque-Musée Fornay, Paris.
Page 109: April 1, 1998, photo of Joy perfume by Jean Patou. Photo by Robb Kendrick.

INDEX

About the Author
Michael A. Sommers is a writer and journalist. He has a twin sister named Annie. They both like French cheese, which they like to eat with baguettes, cornichons, and *vin rouge*.

Designer: Geri Fletcher; **Cover Designer:** Tahara Anderson;
Editor: Annie Sommers; **Photo Researcher:** Fernanda Rocha